SECOND EDITION

MINDFUL
Learning

This book is dedicated to teachers everywhere because their work matters so much to everyone.

SECOND EDITION
MINDFUL Learning

101 Proven Strategies for Student and Teacher **SUCCESS**

Linda Campbell • Bruce Campbell

CORWIN PRESS
A SAGE Company

For information:

Corwin Press
A SAGE Company
2455 Teller Road
Thousand Oaks, California 91320
www.corwinpress.com

SAGE Pvt. Ltd.
B 1/I 1 Mohan Cooperative Industrial Area
Mathura Road, New Delhi 110 044
India

SAGE Ltd.
1 Oliver's Yard
55 City Road
London EC1Y 1SP
United Kingdom

SAGE Asia-Pacific Pte. Ltd.
33 Pekin Street #02-01
Far East Square
Singapore 048763

Printed in the United States of America.

Library of Congress Cataloging-in-Publication Data

Campbell, Linda, 1948-
Mindful learning: 101 proven strategies for student and teacher success/Linda Campbell, Bruce Campbell. —2nd ed.
    p. cm.
Includes bibliographical references and index.
ISBN 978-1-4129-6692-4 (cloth)
ISBN 978-1-4129-6693-1 (pbk.)
    1. Effective teaching—United States. 2. Cognitive styles in children—United States.
3. Individual differences in children—United States. 4. Learning strategies—United States.
I. Campbell, Bruce, 1945- II. Title.

LB1025.3.C34 2009
371.102—dc22   2008017822

This book is printed on acid-free paper.

08   09   10   11   12   10   9   8   7   6   5   4   3   2   1

Acquisitions Editor:	Carol Chambers Collins
Associate Editor:	Desirée Enayati
Production Editor:	Veronica Stapleton
Copy Editor:	Gretchen Treadwell
Typesetter:	C&M Digitals (P) Ltd.
Proofreader:	Caryne Brown
Indexer:	Sheila Bodell
Cover Designer:	Scott Van Atta

Contents

4. Teaching Diverse Students: Addressing Language, Class, Culture, and Ability Differences in the Classroom **105**

Preface to the Second Edition

This book responds to the insights and helpful suggestions from readers of the first edition of *Mindful Learning*. As is readily apparent, the second edition taps the expertise of teacher, consultant, and author Bruce Campbell. In this edition, over 50 percent of the content is new, reflecting the latest research on improving student learning. Other additions include new strategies, graphics, and an even greater emphasis on the instruction of non-mainstream students. Groupings of strategies have been reorganized into consistent categories, and cross-referencing will help readers find what they are looking for more easily. Please note, the authors appreciate hearing from their readers and welcome continued feedback and suggestions.

Acknowledgments

This book would not exist without the gentle nudging of our editor, Mark Goldberg. Thank you, Mark, for seeing this work through to its completion. Likewise, we are grateful that Corwin Press found this book worthy of publication. Though they are rarely acknowledged, we value educational researchers, since it is their work that informs and inspires us all.

Corwin Press gratefully acknowledges the contributions of the following individuals:

Angela Becton, Teacher Instructional Support Specialist
Johnston County Schools
Smithfield, NC

Nancy Betler, Instructional Support Specialist
Charlotte Mecklenburg Schools
Charlotte, NC

Cathy Galland, Curriculum Director
Republic R-III Schools
Republic, MO

Greg Keith, Middle School Academic Coordinator
Department of Academic Affairs
Memphis, TN

Cindy Miller, Project Coordinator
University of North Texas
Denton, TX

Pattie Thomas, School Improvement Specialist
Talladega City Schools
Talladega, AL

Amy Woods, Humanities Teacher
Bedford High School
Bedford, NH

About the Authors

 **Linda Campbell**, PhD, has worked in K–12 and higher education for 35 years. She has created model programs in efforts to improve student learning and teacher education. Upon founding the Center for Native Education (CNE) at Antioch University Seattle in 2002, Linda has served as the Center's Executive Director. As Director, Linda has launched programs that include the Bill & Melinda Gates Foundation–funded Early College High School Initiative for Native Youth, and she also worked with schools and communities to implement New Path. This is an intergenerational model of higher education funded by Lumina Foundation for Education, where underserved adolescents and adults learn together to increase college success. Before her work with the Center, Linda founded the First Peoples' Teacher Education Program as well as Antioch's teacher credentialing and inservice programs. At the K–12 level, she taught in public schools for 12 years and was employed by the National Education Association as a facilitator of school change. Linda has written articles, chapters, and books, including the best seller *Teaching and Learning Through Multiple Intelligence*, and she is the recipient of several educational awards. She may be reached by e-mail at lindacampbe1148@yahoo.com.

Bruce Campbell, PhD, has over thirty years of experience at all levels of education and has authored numerous articles and books. As a classroom teacher, he developed a nationally acclaimed elementary model that integrated direct instruction, learning centers, and student projects on a daily basis. Bruce currently teaches students with high needs in the Marysville School District, where he also coaches educators new to the profession. He is a frequent speaker at national conferences and has consulted for governmental and educational agencies in all fifty states. Additionally, Bruce has taught educators in countries around the world. His areas of focus are ways to improve instruction and how to spark a love of learning among students of all ages. He may be reached by e-mail at bcampbell@teacher.com.

CORWIN PRESS

The Corwin Press logo—a raven striding across an open book—represents the union of courage and learning. Corwin Press is committed to improving education for all learners by publishing books and other professional development resources for those serving the field of PreK–12 education. By providing practical, hands-on materials, Corwin Press continues to carry out the promise of its motto: **"Helping Educators Do Their Work Better."**

Introduction

This book places ready-to-use instructional strategies into the hands of teachers. Rather than being just a compendium of good ideas for the classroom, the techniques here have been proven through research and classroom practice to strengthen student achievement. Research shows a direct link between how students are taught and how well they achieve. In times of heightened accountability, governmental involvement in education, and increasing student diversity, teachers need, and fortunately have, reliable tools to improve instruction.

Historically, research has played a small role in decision making about teaching methods. During the last two decades, however, a new knowledge base of specific instructional techniques has emerged, yielding consistent results with many teachers and students. This book summarizes that literature and showcases its strategies so teachers are supported in their efforts to improve the learning of all students.

It is not a goal of this book to promote a particular educational trend, model, or theory. All experienced K–12 teachers have encountered scores of innovative theories and reform efforts. Exciting ideas can leap from the pages of a new book or the words of an inspirational speaker into mainstream practice, with scant attention paid to whether track records exist of improved student achievement. Often, reforms spread unabated through schools, regions, and, in some cases, the country. Then, when the innovations fail to deliver as promised, teachers frequently are held responsible for the lackluster results. In reality, they were given little to work with in the first place.

Educational and neuroscientific researchers have observed the phenomenon of theory- or fad-driven educational change. They have noted that many innovations not only lack solid research bases but also ignore classroom practice implications and processes (Diamond & Hopson, 1998, citing Stigler & Bruer; Ellis, 2005; Ellis & Fouts, 1997; Grossen, 2000). When innovations skip over instruction, the heart and soul of any improvement effort is neglected and reform is unlikely to succeed.

A lack of focus on instruction is currently evident in the standards reform movement. While state standards and the No Child Left Behind legislation draw attention to issues of student achievement, little thought (for better or worse) has gone into classroom processes that meet the increased achievement goals. In this new era of heightened accountability, school administrators and teachers are analyzing student data and seeking ways to meet children and youth's academic needs. Teachers everywhere, regardless of their school's educational model or legislative demands, want to teach effectively so their students will benefit.

One way to improve achievement is to seek out the knowledge and tools that make learning meaningful, memorable, and effective. This book puts such tools into teachers' hands. It summarizes the literature on key aspects of instruction and provides 101 research- and classroom-substantiated instructional strategies.

We have titled this book *Mindful Learning* for specific reasons. To us, being *mindful* means using proven classroom practices that have worked on other occasions and are most likely to work again. It means meeting students where they are by tapping their existing background knowledge, respecting their diversity by varying instructional processes so all learn successfully, and acknowledging gains with meaningful forms of assessment. Being mindful means making informed, professional decisions about how best to teach, and balancing enthusiasm and personal opinion with research-based strategies so that consistent results can be realized. We intentionally use the word *learning* instead of teaching in the title because student learning should be at the forefront of all efforts to improve education.

The suggestion of basing one's practice upon research does not imply that teachers never innovate. Teachers and students work, creatively and intuitively on many occasions, but it is also true that there are many times when research-tested practices will boost student learning the most. The same holds true for those in other professions. Doctors, mechanics, pilots, and architects rely on professional knowledge to attain predictable results. Being mindful as teachers means putting our professional knowledge base to effective use. We can combine our commitment to children with knowledge and skill to make American education the best in the world.

Where did the techniques in this book come from, and why were they chosen? The book's 101 strategies were derived from two primary sources: the cognitive sciences and educational research on effective instructional practices. The cognitive sciences have recently yielded important insights into how to improve learning. This research influenced key themes and three chapters in this book: engaging student background knowledge, immersing students in active learning, and addressing student diversity. Several instructional strategies are described for each of these three topics; the research that warrants their inclusion in classroom practice is also explained. A brief introduction to the cognitive sciences follows below.

THE NEW SCIENCE OF LEARNING

The last four decades have witnessed a revolution in the study of the human mind. In the late 1950s, a new, multidisciplinary field emerged, that of the cognitive sciences (Bransford, Brown, & Cocking, 2000; Diamond & Hopson, 1998; Gardner, 1985; Willis, 2006). Made up of psychology, linguistics, philosophy, computer science, neuroscience, and anthropology, the cognitive sciences have delved into the complexity of thinking and learning.

Much of the research on learning emerged from studies of the development of expertise, the acquisition and transfer of knowledge, problem solving, and teaching effectiveness. We are gaining insight into the physiological, cultural, metacognitive, emotional, interpersonal, and dispositional aspects of learning. More recently, innovations in neuroimaging and brain mapping with PET scans, fMRIs, and other technologies have become available. These allow us to see areas of the human brain in real time when involved in discrete learning tasks. However, while these studies are fascinating and provocative in implication, the depths of human cognition are not yet well understood. As a result, we limited the strategies from cognitive science researchers to those that have demonstrated the ability to improve student achievement. We theoretically agree that the potential of the human mind is vast but avoid making sensationalized claims about any strategy in this book.

Neuroscientists and educational researchers likewise caution educators about embracing unproven brain-based methods that far exceed their scientific basis (Bransford, Brown, & Cocking, 2000; Damasio & Damasio, 1993; Ellis & Fouts, 1997; Miller, 1993; Sylwester, 1995, 2000; Viadero, 2007). As medical neuroscientist Judy Willis (2006) states, brain research results have been unfortunately "misinterpreted and misrepresented by nonscientists. Every day there are new claims of ways to improve learning and memory from herbs and vitamins to meditation and hypnosis" (p. ix). Many of us can also recall the oversimplification of the right- and left-brain research and the related and erroneous calls for educational change. Essentially, all learning cannot be anything other than brain-based.

Such cautions are mentioned not to discount this book but rather to situate it in the context of what is known about learning at this time. Fortunately, there are reliable theories and strategies that are helpful in the classroom. For example, as we explain in the pages ahead, it is clear from cognitive research (and from every teacher's daily experience!) that different people process information in different ways. No single method will work for all students all of the time. It is important to be intentional about accommodating "difference" in instruction.

This fundamental fact gave rise to this book's offering more than 10, 30, or even 50 strategies. We chose 101 so that educators can choose, adapt and refine several approaches as appropriate for their students. We also explicitly address ways to respond to student differences throughout the pages ahead. Further, another visible contribution of the cognitive sciences to this work is the chapter on engaging students' prior knowledge and another on experiential, active learning approaches for the classroom.

We agree with Daggett and Nussbaum (2007) that the cognitive sciences will have increasing significance for education. In the years ahead, we will probably gain a deeper understanding of how students learn, why some of them struggle and ways to assist, and how to tap the potential of the human mind in the classroom. As the tools of science improve and research continues, we will have even more certainty about how best to teach and how our students— and ourselves—can realize mindful learning.

BEST PRACTICES

Best practice is another educational concept that has been used widely without a clear definition of the concept or reference to a solid knowledge base. What are best practices? Who determines what is best? Best for whom? Are there best practices that work for all students regardless of background and cultural differences? Might the terms "promising practice" or "emerging best practices" be more appropriate?

We do not claim that the instructional techniques in this book represent "best practice." Instead, we searched the literature for research-tested practices that resulted in student achievement gains. What literature was used? The 101 strategies were distilled from three sources: (a) educational meta-analyses of instructional techniques; (b) studies conducted by educational agencies, teams, or individuals; and (c) cognitive scientists who have researched learning and its enhancement. Reference lists are offered at the end of each chapter for readers interested in accessing these resources themselves. Additionally, each chapter begins with a condensed literature review that explains the rationale for the inclusion of each strategy.

It is also worthwhile to point out that not all the techniques in this book are new. While reform movements tend to emphasize cutting-edge initiatives, contributions from familiar researched techniques are also noteworthy. As the knowledge base about effective teaching grows, it should integrate worthwhile discoveries from the past. It is unlikely that many in medicine would shun the Salk vaccine and risk an outbreak of polio simply because the research occurred decades before.

As the reader peruses this book, please note that we are not implying that each technique will yield substantial gains with every student. What we are saying is that research can identify which teaching practices are most likely to produce the desired results. The book's 101 strategies were selected, in part, as a reaction against educational fads that come and go with little to justify their presence. At the same time, we are well aware that research does not necessarily capture all that is valuable in teaching and learning. There may be enhanced attitudes, values, and engagement processes that studies overlook but that readers and their students encounter in the classroom.

WHAT THIS BOOK INCLUDES

The content, format, and conceptual framework of the book were carefully considered. An array of practices are offered for the range of aptitudes, interests, and diversity of contemporary classrooms. Both research and instructional practices are featured in each of the five chapters. The strategies are displayed in a simple, numbered, easy-to-access format. One strategy is described per page; in some cases, multiple examples of an individual strategy are given. While the literature base that supports the inclusion of the techniques can be read in a short time, annotated resources are included in each chapter and references are at the back of the book, for those who desire additional information.

Chapter 1 summarizes the research on prior knowledge and gives 17 instructional approaches for enlisting background knowledge to improve student learning. Chapter 2 reviews the importance of active learning in the classroom, with 27 strategies to offer students many opportunities for experiential, hands-on learning. Chapter 3 discusses the gender-related research on student achievement and outlines 20 instructional approaches to enhance the achievement of both males and females. Chapter 4 highlights effective ways to respond to the diversity among our students. Its 20 strategies address culture's influence on learning, English language-learning, socioeconomic class and learning, and inclusive approaches. Chapter 5 considers performance-based assessment and provides 16 strategies for documenting student achievement.

A simple conceptual framework unites the book's five chapters. As stated previously, though, we are not promoting new educational programming, theories, or jargon. Instead, we want to make explicit the simple teaching and learning cycle that the 101 strategies support. Chapter 1, "Beginning With What Students Know: The Role of Prior Knowledge in the Classroom" is placed first because it is critical that teachers know what students bring to the classroom in terms of prior knowledge, life experiences, and perhaps misperceptions of the content. Tapping background knowledge gives us a starting point—a baseline— to determine where to begin our instruction and to later look back on and see how far students have traveled in learning.

Once students' current knowledge base is determined, then teachers can select strategies from the next three chapters to introduce new content and guide student learning. The chapters are entitled "Active Learning," (Chapter 2), "Ensuring Gender-Fair Instruction," (Chapter 3), and "Teaching Diverse Students" (Chapter 4). A single, unifying concept underlies these three chapters. It is to provide classroom approaches that mindfully and respectfully engage diverse students in learning. The third and final step in the book's conceptual framework is the fifth chapter, "Assessing Student Performance." Here, teachers will find several ways to assess student learning and to involve students in improving their learning through self-assessment.

THE QUESTION THIS BOOKS ANSWERS

This book responds to the question, "How can I improve the learning of my students?" The 101 techniques included here have proven track records with female and male students and with students of diverse ages, languages, abilities, and socioeconomic status. Teachers of every grade and subject will find strategies to apply or adapt to their circumstances. We recognize that teachers may have to adjust the level of a strategy to fit Grade 1 or 4 or 9, but teachers are good at that when they have clear material. We also understand that no one can use all 101 strategies or do all that is suggested all the time. Teachers are encouraged to focus on those strategies of particular importance to them and appropriate for their classrooms.

This book underscores the centrality of quality instruction in improving achievement. The demands of No Child Left Behind ideally should not interfere with good instruction. Though there are and will continue to be many external demands on our time and effort, effective teachers can increase their efficacy by being lifelong students of learning. Part of being a student of learning includes knowing how, when, and why certain strategies work in the classroom. Just as we endeavor to teach students important skills, knowledge, and attitudes, we can model such skills, attitudes, and knowledge ourselves by using research to guide our efforts. Today, as challenges increase both inside and outside the classroom, so has the available research on what works. One teacher in one classroom when supported with effective instructional strategies can make a profound and lasting contribution to the lives of students.

1

Beginning With What Students Know

The Role of Prior Knowledge in Learning

You've probably watched televised ice skating competitions and heard announcers wax rhapsodic about double axles or triple Lutzes. Perhaps the distinctions among these skating feats escaped you. Unless the announcer explained the movements or you figured them out for yourself, it is likely your confusion remained during and after the competition.

This experience is reenacted in our classrooms daily. Many students lack adequate prior knowledge to extract meaning from instruction. Yet we often make assumptions that they come to class possessing the skills and information to learn what we teach. Some research suggests that this assumption is erroneous and that learning is influenced as much by students' prior knowledge as by the new instruction they receive. Attention, then, needs to be paid to this fundamental aspect of the learning process.

Students, of any age, bring beliefs and life and academic experiences to the classroom that influence what and how they learn. At times, such prior knowledge facilitates learning by creating mental hooks that serve to anchor instructional concepts. Conversely, the acquisition of new content can be thwarted if it conflicts with students' preexisting misinformation. As a result, the role of prior knowledge in learning is paradoxical: it can lead to success and failure in the classroom. Consequently, teachers and students alike can benefit from taking time before instruction to identify what is known or, more accurately, believed to be known about a topic. Many strategies can tap students' prior knowledge. Later in this chapter, several are described.

WHAT ROLE DOES BACKGROUND KNOWLEDGE PLAY IN LEARNING?

Piaget (1968) disagreed with the *tabula rasa* notion of the child's mind. Instead, he proposed that young children gradually develop cognitive structures to make sense of the world. By the time they enter school, students have constructed informal theories about how things work, about themselves, and about others (Bransford, Brown, & Cocking, 2000; Carey & Gelman, 1991; Donovan & Bransford, 2005; Gardner, 1991). One example of a common childhood theory is the distinction between living and nonliving things. Some children perceive movement as a way to distinguish what is alive and what isn't. Since people move, they are alive, while plants are not, because they are stationary. In the classroom, children's conceptions about living and nonliving categories, or any other topic about to be taught, can be activated. When this is done, teaching shifts from transmitting knowledge to blank, absorbent minds to refining restructuring and building upon preexisting notions.

When preparing for instruction, most of us focus tremendous effort on the content we will teach. Often, less planning and instructional time is dedicated to accessing preexisting knowledge. This oversight can have significant implications. If preconceptions are not engaged, children may fail to correctly grasp new concepts or give up on a subject altogether. One simply needs to consider the prevalence of the notion that some people are good at math while many are not. Such ideas can prevent learning if not addressed. Further, if students' preexisting knowledge conflicts with the new content, the presented material information risks being distorted. For example, studies at all grade levels have shown students' chronic misunderstanding of basic physics concepts. When they attempt to explain the upward toss of a ball, they describe an initial upward force that is balanced at the top of its trajectory, and pulled by gravity back to the earth (Roschelle, 1997).

Physicists, by contrast, explain the ball toss in terms of a single force, that of gravity with positive, zero, and decreasing momentum. Research has shown that errors in solving math and science problems are not random (Roschelle, 1997). Instead, they emerge from students' underlying concepts or homespun theories. Furthermore, when students are asked to produce rote memory answers to questions, they may appear to know more than they do. If asked to apply the concepts to new problems or to give analogies, they may give responses that consist of unconventional and unacceptable explanations. To counteract the potential negative influence of prior knowledge, teachers and students can dedicate time and effort to making thinking visible and malleable.

WHAT DO RESEARCH STUDIES SHOW ABOUT PRIOR KNOWLEDGE?

Background knowledge is the raw material that conditions learning. It acts as mental hooks for the lodging of new information and is the basic building block of content and skill knowledge. In the literature, the term prior knowledge is often used interchangeably with background knowledge. Here, the terms are used synonymously since they mean essentially the same thing. It is interesting to consider how researchers define the concept. Some simply define prior knowledge as what a person already knows about the content (Marzano, 2004; Stevens, 1980) while others have more complex definitions. For example, Biemans and Simons (1996) conceive of prior knowledge as "all knowledge learners have when entering a learning environment that is potentially relevant for acquiring new knowledge (p. 6). Dochy and Alexander (1995) go further by claiming that prior knowledge is the whole of a person's knowledge, including explicit and tacit knowledge, metacognitive and conceptual knowledge.

Another helpful perspective of background knowledge is evident in Australia's Productive Pedagogies efforts. The State of Queensland's Department of Education (2002) refers to "high connection" and "low connection" learning.

High connection learning gives students the opportunity to link their prior knowledge to the topics, skills, and competencies addressed in the classroom. By contrast, low connection learning introduces new information without any direct or explicit exploration of students' background knowledge. Queensland educators are encouraged to teach productively by tapping student background knowledge.

The Australian example is noteworthy. Substantial research has validated the important role prior knowledge plays in students' academic success (Educational Research Service, 2006; Marzano, Gaddy & Dean, 2000; Smith, Lee, & Newmann, 2001). In fact, research has identified "red flag" approaches to teaching that undermine student motivation and learning. These include foregoing connecting new material to students' prior knowledge (Dolezal, Welsh, Pressley, & Vincent, 2003). Such connections are important because students confront new information every day. They must integrate the new material into their existing knowledge, construct new understandings, and revise current beliefs or theories as needed. Students who lack adequate prior knowledge or are not able to activate what they know often struggle to progress in a subject area or school itself.

As educators, we are fortunate to have meta-analyses and other research available on effective strategies. Before considering the findings from these studies, it should be clarified that there are two primary classroom approaches to working with prior knowledge. The first includes tapping or activating pre-existing knowledge. The second approach is that of building or developing new background knowledge. The strategies included in this chapter address both.

Much of the research on background knowledge has focused on basic skills acquisition (Donovan & Bransford, 2005; Marzano, 2004; Strangman & Hall, 2004). For example, we know that reading comprehension (in many subject areas, not just language arts!) increases when background knowledge about a text's content is engaged (Bolin, 2005; Christen & Murphy, 1991; Graves &

Cook, 1980; Hayes & Tierney, 1982; Ogle, 1986; Stevens, 1982; Strangman & Hall, 2004). Successful techniques for tapping prior knowledge need not be difficult. Several meta-analyses (Marzano, 1998; Pressley, 1992; Strangman & Hall, 2004) reveal that simply asking students what they know about a topic before reading or instruction can raise achievement. Likewise in math and science, research has demonstrated that asking students questions about key concepts and/or clarifying them before teaching the content increases achievement (Fuson, Kalchman, & Bransford, 2005; King, 1992; Minstrell, 1989).

Many studies suggest that mathematics instruction should build on students' existing knowledge along with teaching computational algorithms (Ball, 1993; Bolin, 2005; Bransford, Brown, and Cocking, 2000; Carpenter & Fennema, 1992; Carpenter, Fennema, & Franke, 1996; Donovan & Bransford, 2005; Educational Research Service, 2007; Lambert, 1986). This is because students often possess relevant information that can assist them in mastering new content. A case in point is that many children have informal methods for working with math in their everyday lives. Such knowledge can be engaged when the formal symbol systems are taught. Younger students might explain how they know the number of classmates stepping on and off a school bus. Older youth can be asked about financial approaches to buying a car. For those struggling with math using student think out louds and explicit instruction have been shown to enhance background knowledge (Education Research Service, 2007; Gersten & Clark, 2007). It is also important that teachers teach and ask their students to use the language of mathematics and the actual vocabulary encountered in the classroom and text.

Vocabulary plays a fundamental role in any student's knowledge base. In fact, some research suggests that teaching vocabulary is synonymous with building background knowledge (Marzano, 2004). Understanding key words is critical before learners can progress academically. For example, the average number of new words expected to be learned by a middle schooler is around 600 annually while for a high schooler it is 800 (Bolin, 2005; Marzano, 2004). It is easy to see how students can fall behind if they do not learn vocabulary.

Unfortunately, many students do begin behind. Studies of diverse first-grade students reveal that many possess half the vocabulary knowledge as their peers (Graves & Slater, 1987; Marzano, 2003; Nagy & Herman, 1984). Fortunately, all teachers at all grade levels, in all subject areas, can teach the essential words for their disciplines. A benefit of the standards movement is that it has targeted specific words in subject areas which can be the ones taught. Further, it is important that students use and apply the words themselves. Teachers may be interested in the work of Marzano (2004, 2005) and his colleagues at Mid-Continent Research for Education and Learning (MCREL). They identified nearly 8,000 words for common subject areas and suggest that teachers and schools teach 30 key terms per subject area annually. Additionally, the Tennessee State Department of Education (2006) has launched a statewide effort and has posted K–12 vocabulary for core subject areas on its Web site.

The recent emphasis on developing background knowledge by teaching key vocabulary echoes research findings from the cognitive sciences. In addition to the acquisition of facts, learners of all ages need to be taught key organizing ideas or generalizations of the topic or discipline at hand (Bransford et al., 2000; Diamond & Hopson, 1998). Big concepts or categories provide the glue for factual understanding, accommodate in-depth learning, and allow students to transfer and apply what they know. If a conceptual framework is lacking, students will be left to rely on their own preconceptions about how the world works.

Many researchers maintain that a significant purpose of education is to correct students' erroneous notions (Bransford, Brown, & Cocking, 2000; Donovan & Bransford, 2005; Gardner, 1991; Strangman & Hall, 2004). Attempts to make sense of the world, self, and others begin in early childhood and such homespun theories are not often correct. Subsequently, they can have consequences in K–12 education. Strangman and Hall (2004) report several studies that show that when students do harbor misperceptions, prior knowledge activation can actually impede new learning. Preexisting ideas can distort or interfere with the new content. If this occurs without intervention, students can fare poorly on tests and disregard information that conflicts with theirs. When teachers encounter misperceptions they should find, or help the student to discover, thoughtful ways to correct such ideas. Of course, establishing the conditions that enable student thinking to be revealed is no small task in and of itself. A positive, inquiry-based classroom environment is a prerequisite for students to share what they think they know. At the same time, creating a level playing field of knowledge for all students matters. Even a shallow amount of correct prior knowledge does much to improve learning in the short run and allows for greater depth at a future time (Marzano, 2004).

It would be a mistake to think that prior knowledge's only influence on learning is negative. This is not the case. Learning ultimately begins with the known and proceeds to the unknown. Connecting everyday experiences with classroom topics and intentionally engaging preexisting knowledge with new classroom content can promote meaningful and lasting learning.

A large number of studies on the topic of prior knowledge has focused on improving reading comprehension. This lens into prior knowledge emerged because of the need for students to be able to read to learn in all subject areas. Several approaches have been identified as capable of improving students' comprehension of informational texts.

Direct instruction strategies have shown much promise with diverse elementary, junior and high school students (Graves, Cooke, & Laberge, 1983; Stevens, 1982; Strangman & Hall, 2004). Examples of such techniques include vocabulary instruction as mentioned above, introducing difficult concepts contained in a text before reading, and providing plot and character synopses before reading narrative text.

Of course, there are many alternatives to direct instruction as well (Education Research Service, 2006). Such strategies include individual reflection and recording, interactive discussions, peer question and answer sessions, and, importantly, connecting concepts in a text with one's prior knowledge. Students can also compare and contrast new and existing knowledge. Patchen (2005) also talks about diversifying classroom groups to encourage participation among all students and to pose questions to everyone that are answerable. For example, teachers can ask students' for their opinions of classroom readings to avoid right or wrong response constraints.

For culturally diverse students, previewing can be especially vital in achieving academic success. Sandefur, Watson, & Johnston (2007) explain that some students need explicit frames of reference. The authors recommend "frontloading" the development of prior knowledge through visual media or simply talking about the issue.

It goes without saying that background knowledge is contextual and culturally construed. A challenge for teachers is to insure that all students reach the same high standards while communicating respect for their students' uniqueness. Building a common knowledge base among all students is challenging, and yet, as researchers have shown, good teaching remains good teaching in most environments (Ellison, Boykin, Towns, & Stokes, 2000; Williams, 2006). For example, Williams (2006) explains whether culturally relevant teaching differs from good teaching: "Culturally relevant teaching includes all that is considered good teaching but also takes the learner's cultural background into consideration, building on the student's experiences and affirming his or her cultural identity" (p. 12).

Teachers can strike a balance between commonality and diversity in their classrooms. All students can be helped to acquire the same skills necessary for contemporary society, and at the same time, respect for their diversity can be affirmed. What are strategies that teachers can use to engage students' cultural knowledge? Such techniques consist of asking open-ended questions so that students are not limited to right or wrong responses or approaches (DomNwachukwu, 2005; State of Queensland, 2002).

As the brief literature review reveals, background knowledge plays a significant role in student achievement. There are myriad such strategies for teachers to employ in their classrooms. Building on direct techniques consists of immersing students in hands-on experiences such as science labs, mentoring, or field trips. Building approaches also include teaching key academic vocabulary, previewing what is ahead, and explaining difficult concepts before they are taught in depth. Activating or tapping prior knowledge strategies includes reading, writing, discussing, thinking out loud, and visual cues or organizers.

Engaging students' preexisting knowledge or misperceptions offers teachers one way to informally diagnose their students' baseline. This can then serve as the critical first step in the learning cycle of the classroom. By meeting students where they are, teachers can make informed, strategic decisions about the content to be taught.

In the pages ahead, there are 17 research- and teacher-tested strategies for activating and building student background knowledge as well as resources for finding more.

#1: THE KNOWN AND THE UNKNOWN

A simple strategy for tapping student prior knowledge is the use of Known and Unknown charts. At the beginning of a lesson or unit, introduce the new topic or concept to the class. Using butcher paper or the blackboard, draw a chart with two columns. The first column should be labeled The Known and the second The Unknown (see Figure 1.1). To elicit student prior knowledge, ask students open-ended questions about the concept, such as: What makes stories interesting to read? What makes plants grow? Student responses should be logged as appropriate in either column. Students can also be asked what they are curious about and those responses placed on the chart as well. If content is not suggested by the class, inform students of the additional topics that they'll cover. Ask them where to place those concepts on the chart as well. This will give students a quick preview of what is ahead in their studies. During this activity, teachers should be on the lookout for any student misperceptions. If misinformation is volunteered, reframe the student statement as a question and write it in the second column. Doing this will avoid reinforcing erroneous notions.

This strategy can help teachers fine-tune the content of their instruction. When teachers assess what students know, they can strategically allot time to the areas of greatest need.

Figure 1.1　The Known and the Unknown

The Known	The Unknown

Known and Unknown charts can also be completed individually by students as long as the charts are reviewed and any misperceptions are pointed out. The charts can also be saved or posted and referred to as the class progresses through the unit. Some teachers have students check off items as they are learned. Others put the charts away the day they are created and bring them out at the end of a unit for students to compare and contrast their prior knowledge with current content knowledge.

#2: THINGS I KNOW, THINK I KNOW, WANT TO KNOW

Make a chart and divide it into three sections titled, What I Know, What I Think I Know, and What I Want or Need to Know (KTN) (see Figure 1.2). After informing students of what they are about to study, ask them to brainstorm what they think they know and want to know about the topic. Ask contributors to identify the appropriate column for their suggestions. List the suggestions, while once again as in Strategy #1 noting any that reflect misinformation. Put the misinformation into the column titled What I Think I Know.

Figure 1.2   KTN Chart

What I Know	What I Think I Know	What I Want or Need to Know

A good sequence for the KTN is to first develop a whole-class KWL chart, then small group charts, and then individual charts. This scaffolds students' skills at learning how to tap their own background knowledge. Check the charts for any misinformation and tell students that they'll learn content that clarifies any areas of confusion.

#3: WHAT I KNOW, WANT TO KNOW, AND LEARNED

Three-column charts can be drawn that are similar to KTN, as shown below in Figure 1.3. A teacher or student serving as the recorder can log what classmates say they already know about an upcoming lesson, what they want to know, and what they learned (KWL) after instruction. Although this method is similar to the one above, it differs in that it records the entire process of learning from prior knowledge to completed studies. Just like the KTN, this chart can be scaffolded from whole group to small group to individual.

Additional columns are sometimes added to turn the KWL chart into a learning log. For example, a fourth column might be labeled "What Else I Want to Learn," then a fifth could be labeled "How I Used the Information." It is advisable that students chart the new vocabulary they acquired to reinforce their background knowledge for future studies.

Figure 1.3   KWL

What I Know	What I Want to Know	What I Learned

#4: GETTING ORGANIZED GRAPHICALLY

Students' prior knowledge can be tapped with simple graphic organizers. Graphic organizers are diagrams that visually display information. Depending on their structure, they can show relationships among data, such as hierarchies or subcategories, to use for many purposes as they assist students in visually organizing information and isolating important details. For the first example in Figure 1.4, students were asked to write a given topic in the center of a piece of paper (Step A). Next, for Step B, they brainstormed topics they knew were related to the topic in Step A. As they progressed through the unit, they added concepts to their organizers as shown in Step C.

Figure 1.4 Graphic Organizer

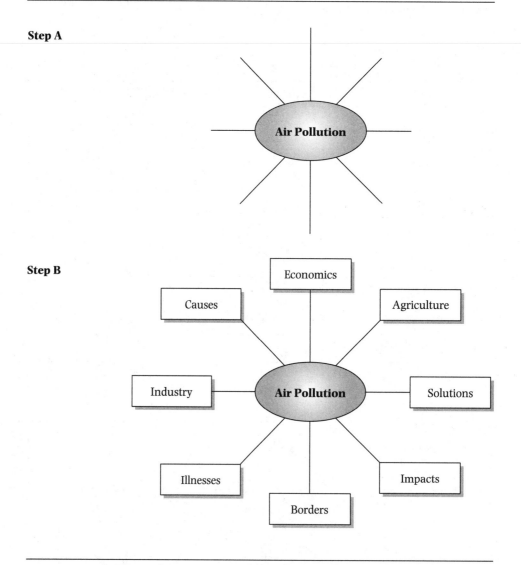

Step C

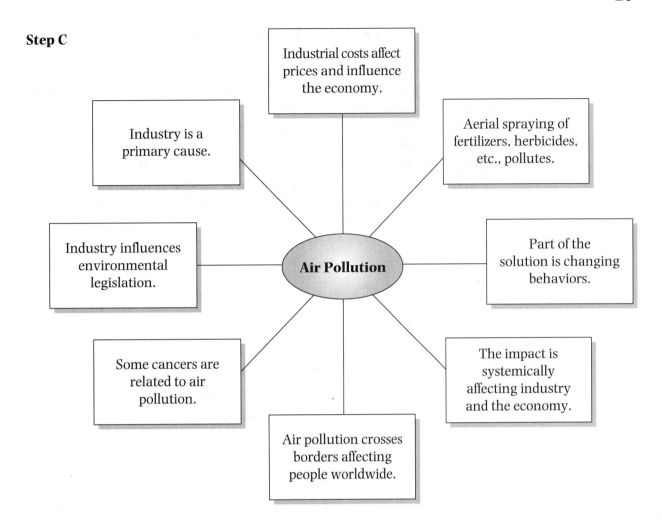

#5: VISUAL SEQUENCING

Background knowledge can be assessed or developed by visually identifying the steps of a lesson, a sequence of events, or a cyclical process. Two templates are provided in Figure 1.5: a flow chart and a cycle. At the beginning of a unit, either give students copies of one of the templates below or ask them to draw what you model on a chart or white board. Next, ask students to identify the potential steps or stages of the process—how one event leads to the final outcome—and to place the steps on the visual diagram. As they progress through their studies, students should correct earlier assumptions and elaborate on each component.

Figure 1.5 Flow Charts

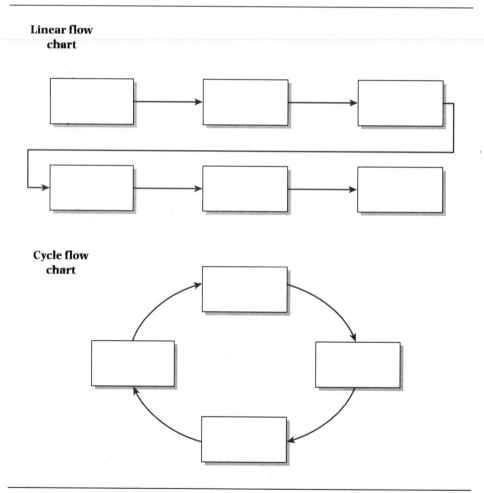

Linear flow chart

Cycle flow chart

#6: VISUALIZING CAUSE AND EFFECT

Students can be asked to explain their assumptions about the causes and effects of a particular event. Later, as they study the phenomena, they can compare and contrast their previous notions with what they learned. Cause and effect charts (see Figure 1.6) are helpful when analyzing a social phenomenon, historical event, or scientific process.

Figure 1.6 Cause and Effect Chart

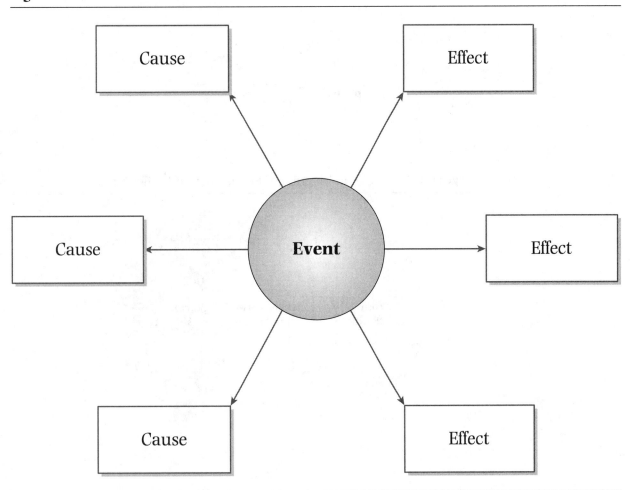

#7: SEEING SIMILARITIES AND DIFFERENCES

Visually identifying similarities and differences among concepts can increase student thinking and understanding. Teachers can use simple graphic forms such as visual analogies in Figure 1.7A or Venn diagrams in Figure 1.7B to engage student prior knowledge, to associate new content with topics students already know, and to compare and contrast their notions before and after instruction. Students can also make copies of these or other visuals and use them to track their learning.

Figure 1.7A   A Visual Analogy of Similarities

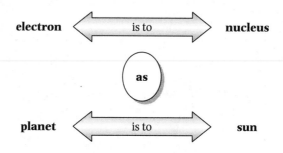

Figure 1.7B   A Venn Diagram of Similarities and Differences

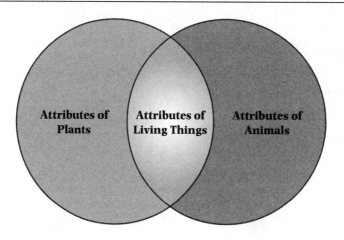

#8: THE WHOLE PIE

Many students benefit from a quick overview of a new concept they are about to learn. An advance organizer taps their prior knowledge to see where it fits into the overall topic. Figure 1.8 below shows a simple way to introduce any concept and its subcategories. In this case, the human body's major systems are identified. The circle itself represents the human body. Each major system is written in the borders of the circle's six sections. Each system is further divided by dotted lines that delineate the subcomponents of the system. Students can be asked to draw the first shape in Figure 1.8. Then questions can be asked to elicit prior knowledge, such as: What is the concept we are considering? Why are we studying this topic? What are its main parts? What are some of its subparts? Students can fill in the details as shown in the second shape in Figure 1.8.

Figure 1.8   The Whole Pie

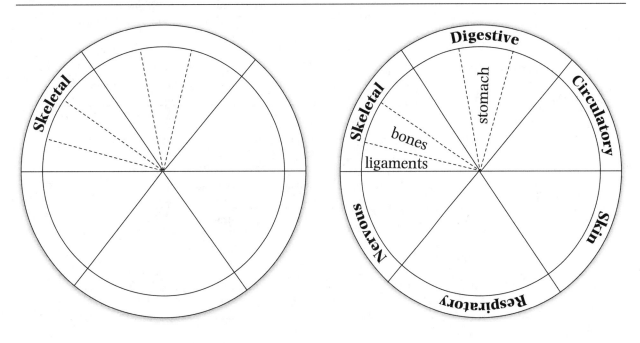

#9: SPEAKING CATEGORICALLY

This teaching strategy is the opposite of #8. Rather than working from the whole to the parts, this strategy proceeds from the parts to the whole. To begin, put the topic you are about to teach in the middle of a blackboard or on a piece of chart paper. Ask students for associations and log their responses nonsequentially around the concept. For example, in Step A, students brainstormed modes of transportation. Next, in Step B, they identified categories that emerged from their previous associations. In Step C, the categories were specified.

Figure 1.9 Visual Brainstorming

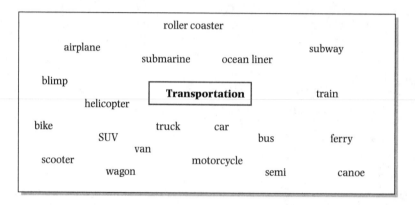

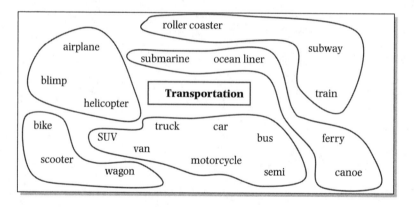

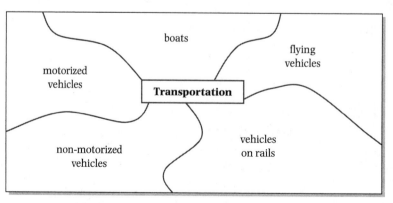

#10: COMMONLY SHARED EXPERIENCES

The first nine strategies in this book suggested ways for teachers to tap student background knowledge. By contrast, the suggestions below offer examples of developing or building prior knowledge through shared experiences. Such events expand the range of students' life experiences and can capture their interest for a new unit of study. Perhaps one or more of the following might be appropriate for your classroom:

- Give a Demonstration
  Example 1: When introducing a new writing convention, first read a letter you have drafted that contains a few mistakes. As in a daily oral language activity, ask students to identify the errors, explain why they were wrong, and offer corrections.
  Example 2: If you are teaching an historical event or geographical feature, begin by showing students a timeline, illustration, map, or globe.

- Introduce a New Topic From Your Personal Experience
  Example 1: In literature, describe how the story relates to an event in another book that struck you or to an experience in your own life.
  Example 2: In math, explain how you use the skills about to be taught in everyday life. Ask the class how they already use them outside of school.

- Read a Brief News or Magazine Article
  Example 1: For language arts, newspaper articles demonstrate parts of speech, stylistic elements, conventions, purposes, and categories, such as editorial opinions, question-and-answer columns, or letters.
  Example 2: For social studies, read an article and compare it to a historical event. For example, show how a current conflict resembles a past war or a current leader compares with a previous one; or, point out differences and similarities in past and current social issues. Similar efforts can also be made with topics in science, art, and math classes.

- Show a Movie or Video Clip, Cartoon, or Web Site Content
  Example 1: For a math lesson, show a video clip of people using math skills.
  Example 2: For a health lesson, show content from a Web site that addresses the importance and social implications of the concept students are about to learn.

- Tell a Story

  Example 1: Use a picture book, legend, or fairy tale as a metaphor for content you will teach.

  Example 2: Aesop's (n.d.) fables illustrate many moral and mathematical issues.

  Example 3: Sharing biographical stories about real people in the past can introduce historical periods.

- Preteach Vocabulary

  Example 1: Preteach vocabulary words selected from the classroom materials students use.

  Example 2: Ask students to identify words new to themselves and give class time for them to teach one another the vocabulary in small groups. Game formats can spark enthusiasm.

- Invite Community Experts or Groups Into the Classroom

  Example 1: Ask students, colleagues, or other adults to identify local community experts who might visit your classroom and explain to students their relevant life and/or professional experiences on the topic you'll teach.

  Example 2: Contact established local organizations or performance groups for speakers or assemblies. These include arts organizations, postsecondary institutions, chamber of commerce, media, and businesses.

- Provide Experiences Outside the Classroom

  Example 1: If resources allow, take students on a field trip to introduce a new topic. Students should be prepared for such an event by knowing appropriate behaviors and what to look for ahead of time. Debrief key points afterward.

  Example 2: Mentoring and tutoring can powerfully expand students' knowledge. Many colleges and universities have student clubs or groups that work with children and youth, as do local volunteer agencies.

#11: CHARTING A COLORFUL COURSE

This process elicits and builds background knowledge simultaneously. To begin, think of five questions about the content students will learn. Write one question each on five large sheets of blank newsprint paper. Hang the sheets on the walls at various points around the classroom.

Divide students into groups of four to six and give one person in each group a marker that differs in color from those given to the other groups. Assign each group to begin at one of the five charts. While at their charts, the groups brainstorm responses to the posted questions; one or more group members can summarize the group's responses on the newsprint.

After two minutes, signal the groups to move to the right to the next chart. Once again, they brainstorm responses to the questions and log them on the second chart. The process continues until each group has brainstormed responses to all five questions.

The groups then return to their original charts, review the content, form clusters of related ideas in big categories of their choice, and eliminate redundant contributions. The groups can also be asked to check for accuracy, identify questions, and summarize what their classmates appear to know. Each group shares key ideas from their charts with the rest of the class.

#12: ASKING THE RIGHT QUESTIONS

Prior knowledge can be easily tapped by discussing any number of questions. To jump-start student reflection on what they know or think they know about the topic, sample questions follow:

- What have we studied before that is similar to this?
- What are firsthand experiences we have had with this concept?
- Who knows something about this concept?
- What are other words we could use for . . . ?
- Who has questions about this topic?
- What does this remind you of?
- What do you remember about this?
- What do you associate with this topic?
- What made you think of such associations?
- Where or when would this be useful?
- Using what we have already learned, can someone walk us through solving this problem step by step?
- How can we extend this to . . . ?
- Where outside of the classroom have you seen others use this?

#13: GUIDED ANTICIPATION

Anticipation guides activate students' prior knowledge about a topic before studying it. Such guides also focus attention on important concepts. They can evoke student reactions, predictions, and corrections. Anticipation guides can be in the form of discussion questions, written checklists, true-or-false quizzes, a list of statements for students to react to, or worksheets. Figure 1.10 supplies a sample guide with sections left blank for students and teachers to complete. Please note, Strategies #22 and #23 also help students anticipate learning.

Figure 1.10   Anticipation Guide

Title of text to be read (provided by teacher):

Main topic (provided by teacher):

What I think I already know about the overall topic:

Statements from the text (two or more are provided by the teacher):

Such statements should evoke student opinions. Students should write whether they agree or disagree with each statement.

Statement #1:

Student opinion:

Statement #2:

Student opinion:

A question I have about the text is:

#14: THINKING OUT LOUD

When teachers explain their thought processes about how they approach a skill or subject content, students can learn to do likewise. Mentoring out-loud thinking helps students identify and replicate strategies that improve their skills and knowledge. Thinking aloud can be used in a number of ways: solving math problems, beginning a writing project, or taking a test. Below are six steps for modeling thinking:

Step 1: Identify a skill or concept you want students to learn.

Step 2: Explain that you are going to think out loud about how you would approach the task. Students should not interrupt you but rather observe the strategies you explain.

Step 3: Think aloud through the task by asking questions about

Emotions: Your attitude toward the assignment and how you might change it, if not positive

Prior Knowledge: What you think you know about the topic or how it is like or similar to other content

Mental Imagery: Your visual images about the topic

Confusing Points: What seems confusing and how to address it

Predicting: Any predictions you might have about the topic or working with it

Planning: Steps to take, along with any alternatives, adjustments, and self-corrections and how you will proceed with the task

Step 4: Afterward, debrief with students the processes they saw you use. Write these on the blackboard and compare and contrast whether all six items in Step 3 were noticed. Perhaps students have other helpful strategies too.

Step 5: Assign a task and ask a student volunteer to model out-loud thinking in front of the class or organize small groups with one or two think-out-loud volunteers in each.

Step 6: Mentor students in their thinking as they work through similar tasks.

#15: USING PRIOR KNOWLEDGE BEFORE, DURING, AND AFTER A LESSON

Linking students' prior knowledge with the new content being studied—before, during, and after a lesson—can increase reading comprehension.

Before a Lesson

Activate prior knowledge by brainstorming or summarizing previous learning that relates to the current topic.

During a Lesson

Help students identify key points, understand new vocabulary, check their predictions, and draw analogies between the new content and what they have learned previously from life and from school. Ask students whether any of their former ideas should be updated.

After a Lesson

Ask students to relate what they learned to their lives and other parts of their schooling. Discuss how they envision applying the new information.

#16: IT'S ABOUT THE WORDS

Before teaching a new unit, review documents that students will use, highlighting key vocabulary in the materials. Next, review state standards in your subject area to see which words appear both in the learning materials and in your state's learning objectives. Identify about ten words that ideally exist in the classroom and state guidelines. If none are evident in both, limit your word search to terms from your classroom materials. Follow the six steps of vocabulary instruction listed in below for an effective way to both elicit and build students' background knowledge.

Step 1: Give a definition and description, explanation, or example of the word.

Step 2: Ask students to restate the word in their own words.

Step 3: Have students visually draw, diagram, or use a graphic organizer to show the meaning of the word.

Step 4: Ask students to use the words in classroom conversations.

Step 5: Periodically, ask students to revisit the words. They might compare and contrast them with others, generate visual analogies, revise their previous descriptions and drawings, and identify word roots that apply to other vocabulary terms.

Step 6: Involve students in games that let them play with the words, such as Jeopardy! or word Bingo.

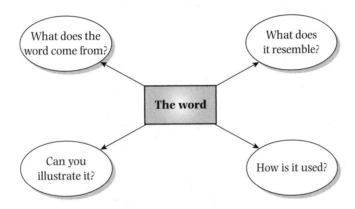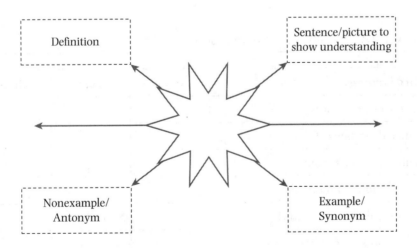

#17: WORD DIAGRAMMING

Many students find it easier to remember vocabulary when they work with words visually and learn their broader context. The examples in Figures 1.11A and 1.11B ask students to interact with disciplinary terms in multiple modes. Such strategies can build students' prior knowledge of key concepts. Note, these simple graphic forms can be used when information does not need to be presented in any order.

Figure 1.11A Word Definition Diagram

Figure 1.11B Word Star

Word Stars can be displayed in a classroom as new vocabulary terms are encountered. If posted, students can refer to them as they progress during a course.

#18: TRACKING PROGRESS WITH WORDS

When students are learning new words, they often like knowing what information the teacher wants. Make copies of the grid below and disseminate one to each student at the beginning of an instructional unit. Students and teachers can respond to each word learning strategy in different colored pens to compare the teacher and student's perceptions of word knowledge and use.

Student Name: _____

Date: _____ Subject: _____

Words to learn:

1. _____

2. _____

3. _____

4. _____

5. _____

6. _____

Figure 1.12   Vocabulary Progress Grid

Word Strategy	Poor	Fair	Good
Spelling of new words			
Written definitions of new words			
Identification of synonyms			
Identification of antonyms			
Use of words in written work			
Use of words in speaking			

#19: MATH DILEMMAS

Students frequently encounter math situations outside of class. If these were brought into school, they could inform the teacher about students' math interests and current levels of background knowledge. At the beginning of a term, ask students to write up math dilemmas they find outside of school. Explain that as the term progresses, you will select problems for the class to solve. Copy the following questions for students to complete when they look for the challenges. Note, the teacher may want to make certain topics off-limits (such as personal budgets) and provide examples such as calculating the amount of waste an person generates in a week, how tall a tree or building is, how much storage a closet $4 \times 6 \times 10$ could hold, the number of grams of fat in common snacks, etc.

Student Math Problems

Step 1: Describe a math problem you encountered outside of class.

Step 2: Explain why solving this problem would be helpful to you or others.

Step 3: Gather the data that are available and needed to solve the problem. Write the data below.

Step 4: Explain how you gathered the data.

Step 5: In one sentence, write your exact question you want answered.

Step 6: Guess the process for solving the problem.

Step 7: Estimate a possible answer.

SUGGESTIONS FOR FURTHER INFORMATION ABOUT PRIOR KNOWLEDGE

David, B. (2005). *How to teach students who don't look like you: Culturally relevant teaching strategies.* Thousand Oaks, CA: Corwin Press.

Bonnie Davis describes her book for teachers from a teacher. Many of the chapters focus on instructional strategies such as providing students with multidisciplinary learning experiences, balanced literacy approaches, and strategic teaching. The unifying theme of the book is how a teacher can support diverse students in part by reflecting on our own view of the world and issues of racial identity. Davis's approach to building background knowledge is to assist teachers in understanding students from other cultures.

Donovan, M. S., & Bransford, J. D., (Eds.). (2005). *How students learn: History, mathematics, and science in the classroom.* Washington, DC: National Academy Press.

This book builds upon its best-selling predecessor, *How People Learn* (1999, 2000), with its groundbreaking synthesis of cognitive science research on learning. This volume, however, moves beyond research to show how the findings on learning can guide instruction. Three subject areas are addressed at the K–12 levels: math, science, and history. Actual lessons are included as models of effective instruction, all of which begin by engaging student background knowledge. This book is recommended reading for teachers of all subject areas because the learning principles it emphasizes are appropriate across the curriculum.

Gardner, H. (1991). *The unschooled mind: How children think and how schools should teach.* New York: Basic Books.

In this book, Gardner explores why children fail to master what schools teach. He hypothesizes that children construct durable "workaday" notions about life, objects, self, and others by age 5 or 6. Because schools typically teach in rote, mimetic ways, students' self-constructed theories endure, preventing in-depth disciplinary understanding from being realized. To dislodge student misconceptions, Gardner suggests ways schools might teach to achieve meaningful understanding.

Marzano, R. (2004). *Building background knowledge for academic achievement: Research on what works in schools.* Alexandria, VA: Association for Supervision and Curriculum Development.

This book makes a case for the use of two approaches, sustained silent reading and subject-specific vocabulary instruction, to help overcome deficiencies in background knowledge that hamper many students' achievement. Marzano provides vignettes of how to implement reading and vocabulary programs throughout the K–12 levels. The book also includes a list of 7,923 vocabulary terms gathered from national standards and other publications. They are organized into 11 subject areas and 4 grade-level categories.

State of Queensland, Department of Education, Australia. (2002). *Productive pedagogies*. Retrieved January 9, 2008, from Department of Education, Training and the Arts, Queensland, Australia, from http://education.qld .gov.au/public_media/reports/curriculum-framework.

The New Basic Project in Australia and New South Wales seeks to improve student learning with four instructional elements. These are connectedness, supportive classroom environments, intellectual quality, and the recognition of difference. Connectedness refers to the explicit linkage of student background knowledge with classroom content. The Web site above illustrates teaching with varied degrees of connectedness between students' linguistic, cultural, and everyday experiences. The site also defines high connected and low connected instruction and provides examples of this and its other core concepts.

Strangman, N., & Hall, T. (2004). *Background knowledge*. Retrieved January 10, 2008, from the National Center for Accessing the General Curriculum, from www.cast.org/publications/ncac/ncac_backknowledge.html

This research-packed literature review not only provides an excellent overview of the concept of background knowledge but also includes extensive Internet resources on the topic. Using reading as their primary focus, Strangman and Hall define background knowledge, identify strategies for tapping and developing prior learning, and explain research studies' approaches and weaknesses. The authors also explore debates in the field.

2

Active Learning

Differentiated Strategies for All Learners

When we are asked to recall memorable learning experiences from the past, those that usually spring to mind are ones that engaged us in multisensory ways. Such moments are remembered because they involved more than our intellects. They involved our hearts and hands as well as our minds in learning and yielded insights that mattered to us then and now. It is unlikely when asked to identify significant educational events that we would remember time spent on worksheets, textbooks, or quizzes. These activities are not particularly memorable because learning relies on active engagement. Students want to see, hear, touch, discover, apply, and reflect on the content, skills, and competencies they are acquiring in order to know and understand.

It comes as no surprise that educational organizations representing core disciplines such as math, science, reading, social studies, and writing promote similar goals for teaching and learning. Reports from the National Council of Teachers of Mathematics, the National Council for Social Studies, the American Association for the Advancement of Science, the National Council of Teachers of English, and the National Association for the Education of Young Children all recommend instructional practices that include experiential, active, hands-on learning (Zemelman, Daniels, & Hyde, 1998; 2005). For example, the curricular position statement of the National Council for Social Studies asserts that "the social studies program should engage the student directly and actively in the learning process" and . . . "offer students a wide and rich range of learning activities" (National Council for Social Studies, 2002).

While the emphasis on learning by doing may be current in the twenty-first century, in all likelihood, active learning was early humanity's essential instructional method (Lorenzen, 2001). When survival was paramount during the hunting/gathering phase of existence, lecturing would have been inferior to youth's learning by observing and being tutored by skilled adults. Centuries later, in ancient Greece, the Socratic method required students to actively interact with each other and the teacher.

More recently, additional philosophers have promoted learning by doing. For example, Rousseau's *Emile* in 1762 emphasized learning through the senses. John Dewey convincingly argued that children should be engaged in an active quest for learning and new ideas. Jean Piaget made it clear that "experience is always necessary for intellectual development . . . the subject must be active . . ." (Labinowicz, 1980). And now, today, educational and cognitive researchers alike agree that learning is not a spectator sport. It requires sensory stimulation, variety, ongoing challenges, and numerous forms of interaction and involvement. Students of all ages crave activity rather than passivity in any classroom.

WHAT DO RESEARCH STUDIES SHOW ABOUT ACTIVE LEARNING?

Active learning encourages student participation in class. It requires more of students than listening and more of teachers than transmitting information. The terms "active learning," "experiential learning," "hands-on learning," and "learning by doing," are typically used interchangeably. In this book, "active learning" encompasses these terms and refers to active, multisensory, and participatory rather than passive forms of student learning.

Active learning theory and research emerge from two fundamental assumptions (McKinney, 2008). The first is that learning itself is an active endeavor. The second is that different people learn in different ways. Researchers from the cognitive sciences address both assumptions.

World-famous neuroscientist Dr. Marion Diamond (Diamond & Hopson, 1998) has spent a lifetime documenting the importance of enriched, multisensory environments in learning. We know from her and other brain researchers that the more ways something is learned, the more memory pathways are developed. For example, Andreason et al. (1999) showed on PET scans that hands-on learning stimulates two different memory systems in the brain that become linked together. These systems recall factual memory and event memory of the hands-on processes. By activating both, students have a greater likelihood of remembering what they studied with less need for rote learning. As neurologist Willis (2006) has observed, when students learn through hearing, seeing, doing, and touching, they physiologically absorb or become the information. As a result in the pages that follow, hands-on, experiential learning strategies are emphasized.

The cognitive sciences have further revealed that though everyone possesses the same neurological architecture, each person is wired to perceive, process, and express talent and learning in highly individualized ways. Perhaps the best known cognitive researcher to underscore this fact is Howard Gardner. His Theory of Multiple Intelligences, introduced in 1983 and refined in subsequent writings, asserted that human intelligence is not a single, unified problem-solving capacity. Instead, Gardner outlined eight autonomous intelligences.

These separate capacities were identifiable in people who suffered some form of brain damage. Depending on the area of the brain where the damage occurred, certain intelligences were diminished while others remained intact. Today, electrological and radiological studies reveal different areas of the brain processing varying types of problems (Gardner, 2003; Willis, 2006).

As the reader is likely aware, the eight intelligences are linguistic, mathematical, musical, kinesthetic, visual, interpersonal (knowledge of others) intrapersonal (knowledge of oneself), and naturalistic (knowledge of the environmental and systems thinking). Gardner never assumed that his theory of intelligence would interest educators. Nevertheless, it has been widely implemented in schools around the world due to its implications for diversifying instructional and assessment methods and for democratizing the ideas of giftedness and being intellectually challenged. As Gardner stated at the 2003 AERA Chicago conference, since "individuals differ in their intellectual profiles, it makes sense to take this fact into account in devising an educational system" (Gardner, 2003).

What's been learned about achievement when instruction taps multiple intelligences, or, phrased differently, when learning is multisensory in nature and actively engages students? It is fascinating to see the significance many research studies attribute to multisensory learning. While reading, writing, speaking, and listening are important, significant gains have been realized when students visually, kinesthetically, emotionally, and collaboratively engage in learning (American Association of School Administrators, 2001; Campbell & Campbell, 1999; Gabel, 2004; Lovelace, 2005; Marzano, 2007; Nuthall, 1999). Five active learning techniques that can be applied across multiple disciplines are summarized below:

Five Active Learning Approaches in the Classroom

1. <u>Vary the sensory processes used to teach the same content.</u> Rovee-Collier (1995) and Nuthall (1999) found that students require at least four exposures to content before it is integrated into their knowledge base. Varying the kinds of sensory exposure to the same content increases student learning. This means incorporating visual, tactile, dramatic, musical, social, and reflective interactions with the information.

2. <u>Use stories, role-plays, debates, and simulations of key concepts.</u> When students observe or participate in a dramatic enactment, their retention of its academic content significantly increases. In fact, student recall has been shown to last as long as a year later, and significant achievement gains have been demonstrated on several measures (Barrell, 2001; Guzzetti, Snyder, & Glass, 1993; Marzano, 2007; Nuthall, 1999; Nuthall & Alton-Lee, 1995). An alternative to role-play is simple storytelling that includes key concepts. In addition, debates that emotionally engage students in defending their position also boost achievement. Storytelling can be done by teachers or community members.

3. <u>Use visual instruction to increase learning (Cawelti, 2004; Marzano, 2007; Nesbit & Adesope, 2006; Robinson & Keiwra, 1996).</u> Such methods

include graphic organizers, concept maps, time lines, flow charts and other forms of spatial reasoning, drawing, mental imagery, model making and watching demonstrations. Second to dramatic instruction in efficacy, visual learning methods boost student understanding and recall.

4. <u>Employ flexible grouping strategies.</u> Since learning is a social endeavor, strategies that promote interaction are often more effective than when students work alone (Brophy, 2000; Cawelti, 1999; CREDE, n.d.; Educational Research Service, 2006; Gabel, 2004; Johnson & Johnson, 1989; Marzano, Gaddy, & Dean, 2000; Patchen, 2005). Students can be organized to work in pairs or small groups whose membership changes periodically. Groups can be formed by language, interests, friendships, mixed academic abilities, or other qualities that promote interdependence. At times, the teacher can also serve as a group member. As with any other technique, collaborative learning should not be overused.

5. <u>Teach students self-directed learning.</u> An ultimate goal of K–12 education is the development of savvy lifelong learners. To do this, students must be actively engaged in managing their learning during the K–12 years. Self-directed strategies can be explicitly taught and applied in any classroom and throughout an entire school. When they are, students prepare themselves for successful futures, and simultaneously, as many studies demonstrate, achieve at higher levels during K–12 schooling (Bransford, Brown, & Cocking, 2000; Brophy, 2000; Cawelti, 2004; Educational Research Service, 2006; Walberg & Paik, 2005). Learning-to-learn skills consist of goal setting, monitoring, adjusting, and assessing progress, time management, research, discipline-based strategies, and general metacognitive problem-solving skills. Such skills can be taught and practiced by an entire class, in small groups, or through individual student projects.

Another rationale for active learning is simply the nature of contemporary society. Today's students are immersed in a fast-paced, multimedia-drenched world. They can access large amounts of information from many sources, decreasing a reliance on teacher-directed classrooms. Educators rather than talking about how certain cultures, languages, and abilities differ from the norm know that student differences are the norm. Multisensory, interactive, self-directed approaches are essential for student and teacher success.

In part because so much data is available with a simple key stroke, we all, children and adults alike, seek meaning and the "pattern that connects." Researchers from both cognitive science and education have emphasized the necessity of learning both facts and "big picture" concepts before students can master content (Bransford, Brown, & Cocking, 2000; Donovan & Bransford, 2005; Educational Research Service, 2006, 2007a; Gardner, 2000; Marzano, 2007; Willis, 2006). This means that students should understand why and what they are learning and be taught the underlying structure or big ideas of a discipline. If not, they risk encountering countless facts like random dots on a screen void of coherence, meaning, and any satisfying picture.

Research studies comparing math instruction in the United States and other countries reveal a shortcoming of the U.S. standards-based system. Our curriculums tend to sacrifice depth for breadth (Educational Research Service, 2007a; Gardner, 2000; Gardner, 2003). As Gardner (2003) observes, "Efforts to cover too much material doom understanding . . . once the decision is made to "uncover" rather than "cover". . . we can take advantage of our multiple intelligences" (p. 9). In classrooms where less is more and students learn conceptual frameworks, connections among facts and procedures, their achievement increases (Donovan & Bransford, 2005; Educational Research Service, 2007a; Marzano, 2003).

Students who stylistically prefer a big picture approach to learning are at risk of underachieving in a fact-based system. This includes many nonmainstream students with "holistic" or "field-dependent" rather than "analytic" or "field-independent" cognitive strengths (Howard, 1987; Kuykendall, 1991, 2004; Ramirez & Casteneda, 1974; Shade, 1989; Tharp, 1994; Witkin, Moore, Goodenough, & Cox, 1977). Holistic or field-dependent students learn best by moving from the general to the specific, while analytic or field-independent thinkers prefer shifting from the parts to the whole. As a result, classroom instruction needs to address both the forest and the trees.

ACTIVE LEARNING IN THE CLASSROOM

Presented with the same teacher and textbooks, students differ from one to the next in their classroom experiences. Active learning lets us reach more of our students more of the time. This is because content can be acquired and processed through multiple pathways.

The following 25 strategies enlist the visual, kinesthetic, auditory, interactive, and self-directed skills of our students. Several also show how to make the big picture or conceptual framework visible so that facts have meaning and coherence. By differentiating classroom processes, we can banish boredom, focus attention, spark liveliness, enhance recall, and, perhaps, instill in our students the joy of learning that drew us to our profession in the first place.

#20: GIVE ME FIVE! AN ACTIVE LEARNING WHEEL FOR TEACHERS AND STUDENTS

The "wheel" in Figure 2.1 can be used in any number of ways. First, teachers can use it as a quick reference for diversifying instruction. Second, the wheel can be posted in the classroom or copies given to students so that they can choose ways to learn during class or for homework. On occasion, the wheel may also generate assessment options. For example, after specifying the knowledge and skills criteria to be met, students might demonstrate their learning through charts, role-plays, journaling, or other active learning options.

Figure 2.1 Active Learning Wheel

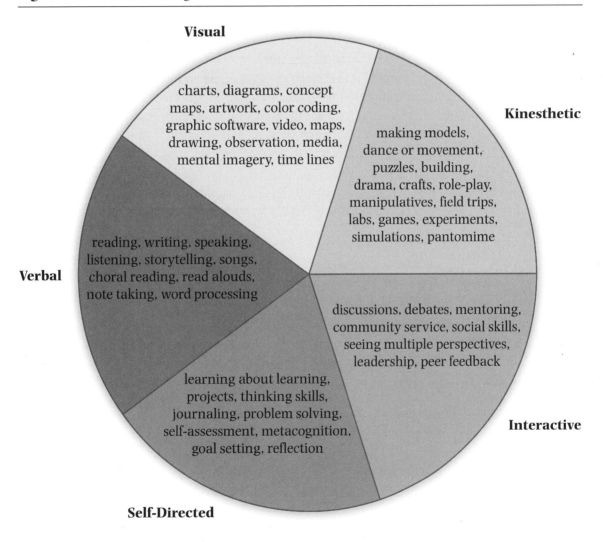

#21: A COLLABORATIVE AND ACTIVE LEARNING SEQUENCE

This cooperative and active learning sequence can be adapted for any subject and is appropriate for adolescents. It integrates four or more active learning methods into a two-hour or two-period time frame. To succeed, it requires student familiarity with small-group work. This strategy shows how teachers can integrate several active learning approaches over time and not attempt to use all during any one single time frame.

Step 1: VISUAL: Give students a graphic overview of concept to be taught (such as Strategy #22 or #23).

Step 2: VERBAL & VISUAL: Lecture for 15–20 minutes on a key concept. Explain how it relates to students' prior learning, the role it plays in the discipline, related key words, its significance, etc. Students begin working on the graphic organizer.

Step 3: INTERACTIVE: Organize students into groups of four or five. Provide them with the needed reading materials, predetermined discussion questions and group roles. Roles can be determined by students or teacher and are shown in Figure 2.2 below. Inform groups that they have 30 minutes to read the text, learn new vocabulary words, and discuss the questions provided.

Figure 2.2 Small Group Tasks and Assessment

Role and Related Group Task	Student Name	Self-Assessment	Group Assessment
Reader: reads out loud and stops at approximately three new words			
Word detective: looks up three or more new terms in a dictionary, the text's glossary, or on the Internet and explains their meaning			
Facilitator: keeps group moving, monitors time and participation			
Note taker: records the group's process, discussion, and learning			
Connector: asks how reading connects to the lecture, prior learning, and group members' lives			
− = Needs Improvement ✓ = Adequate contribution + = Excellent contribution			

Step 4: MULTISENSORY INDIVIDUAL REFLECTION: Inform students the following will be shared in their small groups and turned in. Assign homework or independent class time for students to draw a concept from the lecture and small-group work, compare it with a song, make a simple model, or write about its similarities to other academic topics or life events.

Step 5: INTERACTIVE: Students rejoin their small groups with their reflections. Explain the tasks and roles as follows: Each student takes a turn as a "reporter" describing his or her reflection. The student sitting to the reporter's right asks clarifying questions and solicits comments about the reporter's work. Such questions could be predetermined with copies available for each group if needed. When all have shared, the group selects one reflection to share with the whole class. Group members turn in their individual reflections.

Step 6: INTERACTIVE: The teacher asks group members to assess each other's and their individual contribution. This is done by the note taker's distributing one form from the task in Figure 2.2 above. Each member takes turns assigning a minus (needs improvement), check (adequate contribution), or plus (excellent contributions) for the quality of group work for each peer twice. Above the line assesses Step 3 and below the line assesses Step 5. The students initial their two assessments of one another, and each assesses himself in both areas as well. When all group members have initialed their assessment, the sheet is turned in.

#22: A DAY OF ACTIVE DIVISION

An elementary-level collaborative and active learning sequence is described below. Some teachers dedicate an entire school day for in-depth teaching of an essential skill or concept, as in this case with division. Similar active learning approaches can be applied to multiplication, fractions, or percentages or to nonmath topics such as writing, reading strategies, or the scientific method. Active division can be done as a single class or as a schoolwide project. It requires advance planning for two guest speakers and four learning centers. The learning and goodwill generated by such special active learning days can ripple out in wonderful ways. The daylong agenda is described below.

9:00 Welcome students and guests. Explain the day's agenda and goals.

9:15 KINESTHETIC: Conduct math warm-ups. Ask students to stand and to stretch half their bodies, bend half, crumble a third stand as a whole, etc.

9:25 VERBAL: Introduce the morning's guest presenter (parent, principal, high schooler) who tells a story about a time when division was important. Host question and answer session with presenter.

9:50 VERBAL: Provide direct instruction on one-digit divisors to the class.

10:05 MULTISENSORY: Divide students into groups of three to four for center work on one-digit divisors (perhaps with color-coded items to use). After 20 minutes, students go to the next center for another 20 minutes (perhaps with manipulatives). Guests or others can assist at the centers.

10:45 VERBAL: Reconvene as a class. Debrief what students learned, their questions, and favorite center activities. Provide a break.

11:05 VERBAL: Provide direct instruction on remainders.

11:20 MULTISENSORY: Assign students to center work on remainders for 20 minutes. They switch to second center for another 20 minutes.

12:00 VERBAL: Gather groups together and debrief.

12:10 Lunch

12:50 VERBAL: Read a division story (*The Doorbell Rang* by P. Hutchins).

1:20 MULTISENSORY: Explain creative divisors. Students choose to reenact story dramatically, visually, or through writing and work in small groups.

2:00 VERBAL: Gather for whole-group sharing of creative divisors.

2:20 VERBAL: Introduce second guest speaker who explains how division is used at work. Host question-and-answer session with guest presenter.

2:45 Celebrate day's events, Assign division homework and dismiss.

#23: VISUALLY INTRODUCING A UNIT

Many students benefit from a visual overview of a unit they are about to study. Figure 2.3 below shows one such overview. In this case, students learn that their upcoming unit has six essential questions to answer and the approximate number of supporting facts for each question. Visual overviews can be photocopied and distributed to students as part of their class notebooks or posted on bulletin boards or blackboards.

Options: Depending on the complexity of the content, teachers may decide to complete a visual overview and give it to students as a study guide. Students can then be asked to create a similar one in their own words. Or, students may be given a blank overview that they complete throughout the unit. Additionally, visual overviews help build students' prior knowledge of a topic by showing relationships between the central concept and its components. Readers may also want to refer to Strategies #4–9 and Strategy #23 to see additional visual approaches to improve student learning.

Figure 2.3 Visual Introduction

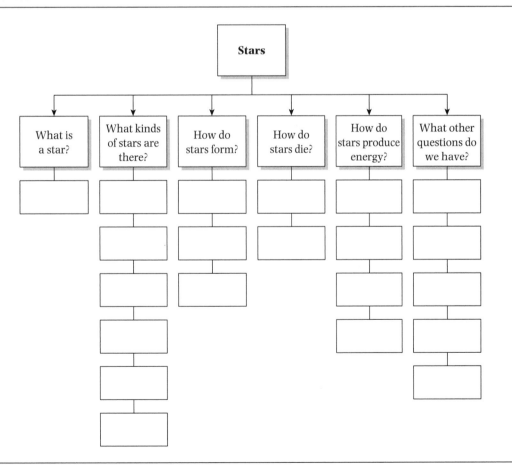

#24: STRUCTURED CONCEPTS

Just as entire units can be visually displayed as in Strategy #22, so can concepts that are part of a unit. Concepts and their subcategories become visible at a glance when presented graphically. Figure 2.4 shows how simple classification trees can be used to display concepts, their subcomponents, and examples.

Figure 2.4   Classification Tree for Concepts

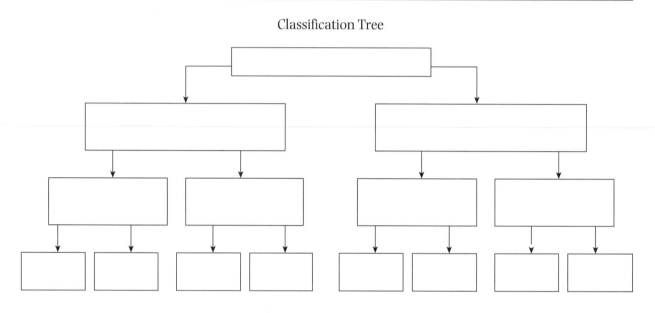

In a unit on the structure of our solar system, students can readily see one concept, the geographic features of the earth, in the following. (Please note, depending upon the content, such trees can visually introduce units as well.)

Classification trees are not only helpful for recording and reading taxonomies; they can also be applied to other data, as the following geography classification tree demonstrates.

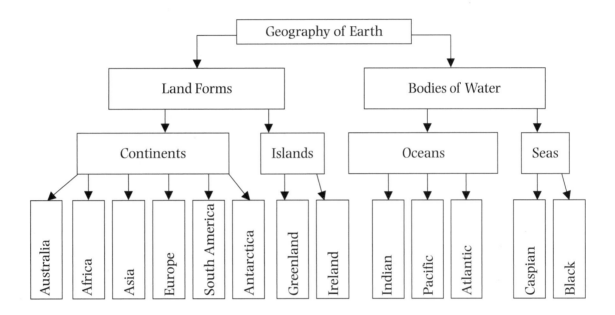

SOURCE: From Linda Campbell, Bruce Campbell, & Dee Dickinson. *Teaching and Learning Through Multiple Intelligences (p. 235). 3rd Edition.* Published by Allyn & Bacon, Boston, MA. Copyright © 2004 by Pearson Education. Adapted by permission of the publisher.

#25: VISUAL REPORT WRITING

Graphic organizers also help students learn skills they need to develop. The sample organizer in Figure 2.5 below walks students through writing a report. It also shows how parts of a report fit together.

Figure 2.5 Visual Report Writing

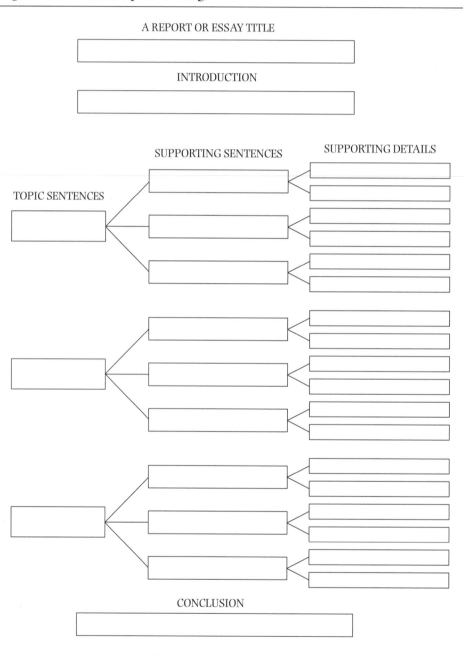

#26: CHARTING SKILLS: ESTIMATION

Simple charts can be developed for any skill students should master. They do not need to be fancy, just helpful! Figure 2.6 explains why estimation is important and gives three approaches to estimating. Students are also asked to generate other strategies so that they can adapt, shape, and make this skill their own. Additional estimation questions provide application and practice. There is no end to the number of simple charts that can be made to help students see and practice subject area skills: comma rules, data collection, collaborative learning, critical reading skills, measuring, etc.

Figure 2.6   Estimation Strategies

Rounding	Front End	Compatible Numbers	Others Developed by Students
236 200 398 400 + 103 + 100 ⎯⎯⎯⎯ ?? ??? 700 (Estimate)	420 324 + 229 ⎯⎯⎯ 81 Estimate = 1) 420 = 400 2) 324 = 300 3) 229 = 250 4) 950 = Estimate	36 ⎫ 12 ⎬ 100 62 ⎫ 89 ⎬ 100 + 20 ⎯⎯⎯ Estimate = 220	

Estimating is an important skill because:

1. It is used more often than calculating exact numbers.

2. It provides referents in determining reasonableness of numbers.

Estimation instructions to give:

1. Estimate the number of first graders at your school.

2. Estimate the number of days you have lived.

3. Estimate how many breaths you take in an hour.

4. Estimate the number of cars in the school's parking lot.

5. Using the chart above, write estimation examples for subtraction.

6. Using the chart above, write estimation examples for division.

7. Using the chart above, write estimation examples for multiplication.

8. Invent your own estimation problems, and switch with another student.

9. Invent your own estimation strategies, and explain them to the class.

#27: VISUAL STORY MAPPING

The organizer in Figure 2.7 helps elementary students identify the characters and events in a story. Using story maps can improve comprehension and recall of narrative text as well as display its common components. For older students, the elements of fiction can be added and concepts such as rising action, crisis, conflict, climax, denouement, etc. can be mapped.

Figure 2.7 Story Map

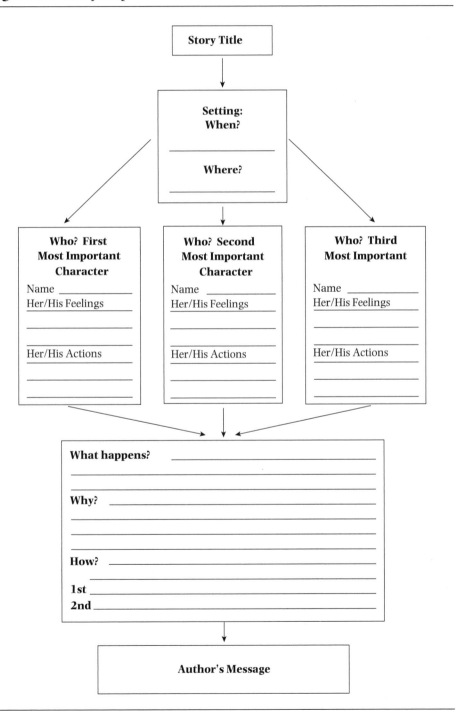

SOURCE: Adapted from I. Beck & M. McKeown (1981).

#28: MASS MEDIA'S MESSAGES

Most students are immersed in a multimedia world and need critical-thinking skills to analyze what they observe, hear, and read. The following activity begins teaching students to critically analyze the ways in which social roles and norms are portrayed by media. Such questions can also be applied to news reports, historical documents, and narrative texts.

Age, Race, Ethnicity, and Physical Characteristics

- Who is represented? Why?
- Who is left out? Why?
- What are the physical characteristics of the key figures?
- What are the messages about age, race, etc.?

Children

- What differences exist in roles for male and female children?
- How are children depicted?
- Who nurtures the children? In what ways?

Masculine and Feminine Characteristics

- How do the portrayals of men and women differ?
- What kind of personalities do men and women have?
- Who would be a role model for others and why?

Careers

- What kinds of careers are portrayed?
- Why are those careers highlighted?
- Analyze the male and female careers.
- How did the lead characters attain them?
- How would such careers be attained in real life?

Relationships

- What kinds of relationships do the genders have?
- Is one more dominant than the other? In what ways?
- Are the relationships realistic or fairy tale–like?

Sex and Violence

- Is sex used to sell a product or a show?
- What consequences of such "selling" might exist?
- How is violence portrayed?
- What is more dominant—the product, the story, violence, or sex?

#29: ACTIVE LISTENING

Students frequently spend classroom time listening to learn, and yet most have not been taught how to listen actively. To improve this fundamental verbal skill, distribute copies of Figure 2.8, Listening Guide, below. Discuss the critical thinking skills it covers. Have students practice using the guide with class lectures, media and political events, guest speakers, and classmate presentations.

Figure 2.8   Listening Guide

Student name: _____

Speaker's name: _____

Title or purpose of talk: _____

_____

Main idea: _____

_____

    Supporting details: _____

_____

_____

Main idea: _____

_____

    Supporting details: _____

_____

_____

Fill in as appropriate:

Vocabulary:	Definitions:
Problem:	Suggested Solution:
Procedure:	Steps:
Opinion:	Rationale:

One-sentence summary: _____

_____

_____

#30: ACTIVE READING

Though reading is often considered a passive process, students must actively engage with text to understand it. Explain to your class that reading is a way to enter into an author's thinking. Students should know their thinking as well as the author's by questioning the content before, during, and after reading. For students to actively engage with text, give them copies of the following questions. They can practice responding to some or portions of the questions as a class, in pairs or small groups, and in journal reflections across subject-matter areas.

Questions Before Reading

- What is the topic?
- Who wrote the text or document? Why?
- What do I already know about it?
- What am I uncertain about?
- Why am I reading it?
- What do I hope to learn or gain?
- What does the cover of the book tell me?
- What does the title suggest?
- What do the chapter headings suggest?
- What do the book's visuals suggest?
- What predictions can I make about the content?

Questions During Reading

- What are the big ideas I am learning about?
- How can I put those ideas into my own words?
- How does the structure of the text help me understand its ideas?
- Can I create images or words for the key ideas?
- What is confusing to me? How can I get clarification on confusing parts?
- Which words are new? How can I learn them?
- How do the visuals contribute to the book's meaning?
- How would I summarize what I have read so far?
- How far should I read before I summarize the main ideas?
- What examples does the author give that explain the big ideas?
- Did my earlier predictions come true?
- What do I think will happen next?
- What am I wondering about?

Questions After Reading

- What did I learn?
- What are some examples?
- How does this story relate to . . . ?
- How does this information expand my knowledge of . . . ?
- What were the most important points?
- Did my predictions come true? Why or why not?
- Are there parts I should reread?
- What do I have questions about?
- What is my opinion of what I just read?

#31: TEXTBOOKS ARE FRIENDS!

Textbooks are not simply collections of random facts, though students may not at first agree. When students understand textbook features, they can use them effectively to learn, explore, and apply subject-area content. Give students copies of Figure 2.9 below and ask them to search for features of their texts. Discuss how each feature supports learning from the text.

Figure 2.9   Textbook Structure

Find the following features of your textbook. Write the page numbers for each item on the left and explain how the feature aids in understanding on the right.

Page	Textbook Feature	What It Contributes to Learning

Title of book

Copyright date

Author information

Table of contents

Organization: Look at the first part of your text. List how it is structured: parts, chapters, sections, subsections, question-and-answer section, or?

Visual components: Look at one section of the text. List how figures, tables, illustrations, or charts are used.

Color coding

Font size variation

Key words, vocabulary

Length of chapters

Index

Reference Glossary

Appendix

Explain why you think the author(s) structured the book as it is. What does this say about how they think students learn?

#32: ACTIVE INVOLVEMENT THROUGH DISCUSSION

Students increase their learning when they are held responsible for the content of lectures or readings in class. The three processes below hold students publicly accountable for learning through whole-class, paired, and teamed approaches.

Two Heads Are Better Than One

1. Pair students heterogeneously. One is Student A and the other B. Give the pairs 5–10 minutes to accomplish three tasks:

2. Both students silently read one paragraph.

3. Student A closes the book and verbally summarizes the information.

4. Student B checks the text's content for accuracy and questions Student A about the summary.

5. The students switch roles and repeat steps 2–4.

Timed Teams

1. Place students in heterogeneous groups of three or four. Have them count off so that each has an assigned number.

2. During a presentation, discussion, or other task, periodically stop and pose a question.

3. Teams have two minutes to discuss and agree on a response and to determine that each group member can speak for the team.

4. Randomly call on teams and a number to respond.

#33: IT'S NOTABLE

Note taking actively involves students in the content of lectures and readings. There are diverse forms and purposes for note taking. Notes help students internalize information and serve as study guides. Sometimes, note taking occurs for a single event or can be added to over time, or developed into a course-long academic notebook. Teachers can suggest the time frame and formats of note taking, including sharing theirs! Options follow:

Figure 2.10A   Teacher Notes

Teacher gives students prepared notes as an example of what is considered important. Students add drawings or graphics and questions.

Teacher Information	Student Visuals	Student Questions
Introducing Water 1. Transparent, odorless liquid 2. Compound of H_2O 3. Most common substance on earth @ 70%		
Properties of water—no other substance appears in three forms 1. solid—ice 2. liquid—rain, oceans 3. vapor—evaporation, steam		

Figure 2.10B Student Notes

Students divide a piece of paper into thirds as shown. On the right side of the page, they record content as suggested and on the left, interact with it personally as suggested. At the bottom of the page, students summarize the entire sheet. For more room, another option is for students to use two blank notebook pages and summarize at the bottom of both pages.

Student Interactions	Class or Text Notes
Simple graphics, drawings, symbols, and illustrations that explain content	Informal outline of class or text content
Metaphors or analogies in slogans, poems, prose, or lyrics	The more notes the better!
Cartoons or caricatures of key ideas	Verbatim noting is discouraged—big ideas, terms, concepts, and examples are needed
Personal reflections	A significant quote or two
Clippings from news reports	A work in progress—continually revised, updated, serves as study guide for test
Summary—from one sentence to one paragraph	

#34: THINKING FROM A TO V

One important aspect of all subject-area instruction is teaching the content knowledge and the thinking processes of that discipline. For example, history seeks to teach students how to think like historians, mathematics how to think like mathematicians, etc. Likewise, science seeks to develop the analytic thinking and skills necessary for scientific endeavors. The mini-dictionary below helps students identify some of the thinking skills involved in scientific pursuits or in any situation when analysis would be beneficial. Students can track which skills they use, which ones they don't use and could, and add more to expand their dictionaries.

A Mini-Dictionary of Analytic Thinking from A to V

- Analyzing

  What are the basic elements of this? What are some underlying assumptions?

- Asking Questions

  What information do we need? What do we wonder about?

- Classifying

  How can we organize these into categories? What common characteristics do they share?

- Communicating

  How can we explain these objects, events, or ideas? What is the best way to get this across to someone?

- Comparing

  How are these items similar?
  In what ways are these items different?

- Connecting

  How does this relate to that?
  What are the cause and effect in this situation?

- Contrasting

  How do these items differ?
  What are the distinguishing characteristics of these items?

- Elaborating

  What would be an example of that? What other ideas or details could we add? How did we arrive at this?

- Evaluating

  What do you think about this and why? How well does this achieve the goal?

- Inferring

  What are the logical consequences of this? What conclusions can we make?

- Interpreting

  How might we explain? How can we describe?

- Measuring

  How can we determine its size?
  What tools can we use to determine its dimensions?

- Observing

  What do we notice?
  What else are we looking for?

- Operationalizing

  How can we put this into action? What do we need to do to study this?

- Pattern Finding

  What is similar about these items? What repetition do you see in this?

- Predicting

  What do you think will happen? How do you know? Why is that likely?

- Sequencing

  How can these items be arranged in a linear way? What should go first, second, and third?

- Summarizing

  How can we retell that in a shortened form? What did we learn?

- Synthesizing

  What emerges when we combine these ideas? Overall, what is evident?

- Verifying

  What evidence is there to support this? How can we confirm or prove this?

#35: THAT'S DEBATABLE

Debates are powerful strategies for improving student learning. Fact-filled and passionate, debates teach a range of thinking skills and deepen content knowledge. The following steps illustrate a process for an informal classroom debate.

1. Choose the topic. There are two common sources: the content being taught or questions students ask. Once selected, write it succinctly for students to copy.

2. Sample topics: Should all students be required to pass a state test for graduation? Should the U.S. have bombed Hiroshima during WWII? Do girls have easier lives than boys? Should society sentence a person to death?

3. Students take sides. Students choose sides or the teacher assigns them. The affirmative side is "pro" and supports the debate's proposition. The negative side is "con" and opposes it.

4. Identify the moderator. This person facilitates the debate and can be selected by teacher or students. She introduces the topic, calls equitably on students to speak pro and con during the debate and brings it to a close. The moderator might be the teacher, a student, or guest. The moderator should research the debate process and behavior, and create an agenda and strategy for calling on students.

5. Identify the opening- and closing-remark students. Students may volunteer or be assigned to give two minute, prepared opening and closing statements. The debate begins with a statement from the pro speaker followed by one from the opposition. Remarks should give an overview and supporting evidence. These students may want to work with their respective teams to integrate their research into their comments and might receive extra credit for their roles.

6. Conduct research. Students research their position and find at least four resources. They may want to identify opposing arguments and be prepared with counterarguments (rebuttal). Figure 2.11 can guide their efforts.

Figure 2.11   Research Template for Debate

Debate Position Statement:				
Source citations	*Pro facts & views*	*Pro examples*	*Counter-arguments*	*Rebuttal responses*

7. Host the debate.

8. Review and assess to learn from one's efforts and improve future debates.

#36: JIGSAW CARDS AND PUZZLES

For students who like to process information in a tactile fashion, jigsaw cards and puzzles are appropriate learning tools. Any type of content can be adapted for jigsaw use, whether it is lecture or textbook readings or pretests from state agencies. As the examples in Figure 2.12 show, students can make jigsaw items themselves. When they do, sets of such cards can be stored for future use.

Figure 2.12 Jigsaws

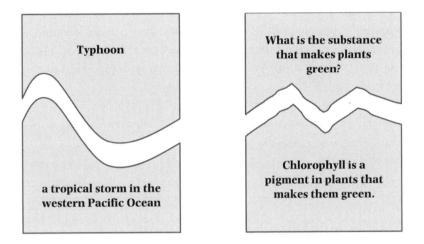

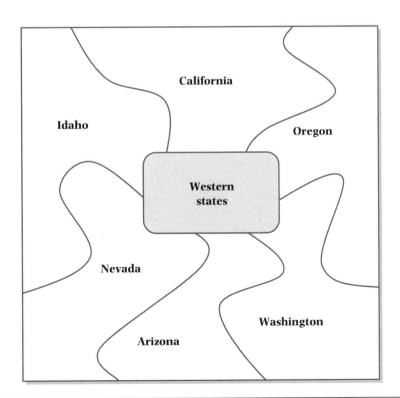

SOURCE: Adapted from Rita and Kenneth Dunn, *Teaching Students Through Their Individual Learning Styles: A Practical Approach*. Published by Allyn & Bacon, Boston, MA. Copyright © 1978 by Pearson Education. Adapted by permission of the publisher.

#37: I'M GAME

Any number of games can be adapted for classroom use and with good reason. Students typically respond to games with increased attention and enjoy their lighthearted competition and multisensory nature. As a result, games are effective at increasing student achievement. They can be motivating for students to make. The simple geography board game in Figure 2.13 is one example. Things to consider when making classroom games include:

- The purpose of the game: to review geography, molecular structure, events, etc.
- Whether the format will be original or commercially adapted, such as Bingo, Jeopardy!, Pictionary, Family Feud, or a spelling bee, etc.
- The types of questions to be asked: short answer, true/false, multiple choice
- How the game will be won
- How players will move or gain points: with dice, cards, or spinners
- Items needed to make the game

Figure 2.13 Geography Game

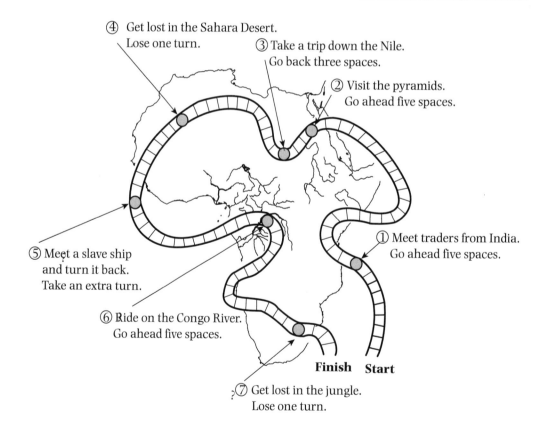

SOURCE: From Linda Campbell, Bruce Campbell, & Dee Dickinson. *Teaching and Learning Through Multiple Intelligences* (p. 114). 3rd Edition. Published by Allyn & Bacon, Boston, MA. Copyright © 2004 by Pearson Education. Adapted by permission of the publisher.

#38: MUSICAL LEARNING

Most of us know from firsthand experience that music evokes images and memories and powerfully influences our frame of mind. Many teachers use music to calm or reward a class, but it is less frequently used for academic purposes. Music, however, can be a multisensory ally in learning. For example, the process below has jump-started many creative writing efforts. Beyond language arts, music can inspire learning across the curriculum.

For Creative Writing

Preparation. Select four varying types of musical compositions that do not have lyrics and bring them to class. Review the elements of fiction with students and clarify the goals of the writing assignment. Explain that the class will listen to brief parts of four musical selections and the compositions will help generate storylines. The students can imagine that they are film producers who were hired to create a movie script to accompany the musical score.

Playing the Selections. Explain that you are going to play two or so minutes of the first selection. It can inspire ideas about the first character and his qualities. Play the selection and ask if two or three students might volunteer their ideas about the first character. Ask all students to quickly jot down key details about their character that the music inspired.

Prepare students for the second selection. Suggest that while listening for a couple of minutes the music can evoke a setting. Once again, students take a minute or two to quickly write key descriptions of settings afterward.

Inform students that the third piece can inspire ideas for a second character who will interact with the first in some problematic way. Play a brief portion of a sharply contrasting third selection. Again, give students a minute or two to capture their inspirations on paper.

Explain that the fourth selection can help students imagine some type of resolution to the problem between the two characters. After a couple of minutes, they can take a minute or two to write key details.

Writing the Story. Teachers may want students to map or graphically outline their stories (see Strategy #27) while the ideas are fresh in their minds. They can later draft their stories in greater detail according to a rubric or other assessment guide the teacher provides.

Music Across the Curriculum

Music can promote learning in many ways. For example, in history, songs of an era can teach social attitudes, events, and values of that time period. Since musical composition follows mathematical rules, math classes can consider the structure of different selections. Many teachers, and better yet students, in any content area can rewrite familiar songs with curricular content. Such songs enliven learning and extend recall, as some students claim, for years.

#39: NARRATIVE PANTOMIME

As the research shows, dramatic instruction can powerfully improve student achievement. Narrative pantomimes are easy-to-prepare dramatizations of concepts or passages in a text. While the teacher reads a short selection, volunteers or the whole class spontaneously use movement to interpret the text. For example, pantomimes can portray completed math story problems, processes such as photosynthesis, accounts of the Underground Railroad, or vocabulary terms. Of course, before reading a selection, the teacher has to find one and encourage student participation. If students are hesitant at first to physically engage in learning, they can be nudged to use their arms and legs while seated. Older students involved in drama may be willing to demonstrate. Usually, however, there are a few extroverted volunteers willing to give the process a try. To assist teachers who have not used this method previously, Figure 2.14 is a pantomime reminder. It can be kept in a lesson plan book or elsewhere to encourage adding this method to instruction.

Figure 2.14   Pantomime Reminder

Pantomime Reminder	
Select Content	1. Skim reading materials for key concepts. 2. Find a short passage to read in class. 3. Add multisensory details—smells, sounds, images, if possible. 4. Add intrigue, tension or conflict, if possible.
Orient Students	1. Explain the academic goal of the activity. 2. Reinforce behavior expectations of performers and audience. 3. Request volunteers or class to participate. 4. Arrange the physical space, if needed. 5. Describe the steps of the process. 6. Show a signal for beginning and stopping.
Pantomime the Topic	1. If the passage is brief, read once so students can generate ideas. 2. Ask mimers to walk to performing area. 3. Ask audience to note helpful interpretations of the content and respectfully support peers. 4. Use signal to begin reading and miming. 5. Read slowly and with emphasis. 6. Repeat any key phrase, if appropriate. 7. Use signal to end.
Debrief and Redo	1. Thank performers. 2. Ask audience what they learned. 3. Ask performers whether the miming strengthened their learning, and if so, how. 4. Ask if an audience member had ideas for "choreographing" the passage, and if so, whether performers might be willing to participate.

#40: ROLE-PLAYING TO LEARN

Another "dramatic" approach to experiential learning is role-play. Role-plays let students assume the perspectives of others with or without props and scripts, and can be easily adapted for any discipline's controversies. A process for role-playing contrasting perspectives in any subject area is described here.

1. Identify a controversy in the discipline you teach that is important for students to consider. Find two short articles or textbook passages that take opposing sides of the topic. Make copies of these selections or refer students to them in their texts.

2. Organize small groups of three students each. Each group assigns three roles: Reader, Perspective #1, and Perspective #2.

3. The Reader reads the two items out loud while the two others read along silently. The group identifies the central conflict and two contrasting views. Perspective #1 and #2 identify which position they'll each assume.

4. Perspective #1 and Perspective #2 discuss the conflict from their points of view. They defend their positions by referring to text-based examples. The Reader steps in to reread any portion of the text that warrants clarification or when students stray too far from their points.

5. After both sides of the conflict have been stated, give the groups the following chart. Ask them to list the main areas of disagreement in the first and third columns.

Figure 2.15   Role-Playing Diverse Perspectives

Student Names and Roles:

Brief Statement of the Conflict:

Perspective #1	Common Ground	Perspective #2
Concern #1		Concern #1
Concern #2		Concern #2
Resolution and Justification		

6. Next, all three students identify areas of agreement evident in their selections or ones that they think exist. They list these in the middle.

7. Last, the groups discuss potential resolutions of the conflict in their articles or that they brainstorm. The groups should first strive to reach a win/win approach. If that is not possible, they justify the resolution that two out of three group members approve as an example of majority rule. The resolution and its justification are included on the form.

8. After students have participated in the role-play, assignments can be given to write essays or letters to the editor, or for students to consider hosting a debate.

#41: A WEEK'S WORTH OF JOURNALING

Another approach to interacting with content, and simultaneously with one-self as a learner, is journaling. Journaling asks students to actively process, reflect on, and embed information in personalized ways. Additionally, when students journal, they develop metacognitive self-awareness—a critical first step toward independent learning.

Some teachers use journaling daily while others use the strategy only after key concepts have been taught. However this strategy is approached, students often want suggestions to jump-start their reflections. The following chart gives students options for any day of the week that they might be journaling as well as nonlinguistic choices for synthesizing their thinking.

Figure 2.16 Journaling Options

Monday Options	Tuesday Options	Wednesday Options	Thursday Options	Friday Options
What was I most or least interested in? Because?	What was the hardest or easiest for me?	What am I most or least certain about?	What was new, and what did I already know?	What did I contribute to the class experience?
A drawing or graphic organizer of my learning . . .	Song lyrics that connect to my learning are . . . because . . .	A movie, news, or TV show addressed the topic when it . . .	An analogy in the form of a sculpture, a dance, a poem is . . .	I could color-code my learning by . . .
My attitude toward the topic was . . . because . . .	Questions I would like answers to are . . .	I learned the key concept of . . . or how to . . .	Mistakes that I made are . . . because . . .	One thing I'll always remember is . . .

#42: STUDENT GOAL SETTING

Learning how to manage and assess one's own learning is of fundamental importance to K–12 educators and, eventually, to all of society. When students have opportunities to assume responsibility for learning, achievement gains are realized. While this may be a short-term goal, students are actually gaining skills to achieve a significant longer-term goal—that of being lifelong learners. As with any skill, however, self-directed learning must be taught. One strategy that begins transferring the responsibility of learning from teacher to student is goal setting. Student-determined goals should address the key questions: why, what, when, where, and how.

Student Goal Setting

Students identify a topic of personal interest that is related to a classroom unit. For example, fourth graders were studying a unit called "How Simple Machines Work." Their teacher explained that all students should identify personal learning goals that reflected their individual interests. At the same time, their goals should remain connected to the topic of simple machines and be doable in one to two sessions of homework.

After brainstorming options, some students chose the following: One decided to compare how much weight small levers could lift and show that information in a word-processed table. Another wanted to identify the types of simple machines used in cooking. A third decided to practice division skills by applying the formula of mechanical advantage, the force of the machine divided by the force of the person. All students completed contract forms below for their learning goals.

Figure 2.17   Contract for Learning Goal

Student Name: _____ Unit Topic: _____
Date: _____ Personal Goal: _____
WHY: I want to learn about this goal because:
WHAT: My tasks to achieve my goal are:
WHEN: The dates I will work on my goal are:
HOW: How I will show what I learned is:
HOW: How I'll determine the quality of my work is:

#43: PROJECT-BASED LEARNING

Project-based learning appropriately transfers part of the direct teaching functions of planning, time management, and review from teacher to student. The result is that students acquire some of the skills needed as adults. This is because most adult work is organized into projects, and all of life requires active, ongoing learning. To have your class actively manage their learning, a project planning form for students follows in Figure 2.18.

Figure 2.18   Student Project Planning Form

Project Steps	Example	Student
1. Goal State your goal.	**1. Goal** *I want to learn how visual illusions work.*	**1. Goal**
2. Question Restate your goal as one to two researchable questions.	**2. Question** *What are visual illusions?* *How do they fool our eyes?*	**2. Question**
3. Outcomes In addition to a three-page paper, identify two or more ways you'll present to class. Review paper and presentation grading rubrics.	**3. Outcomes** *1. A talk for the class* *2. A sample illusion I made.* *3. A handout for the class to see and try making illusions.*	**3. Outcomes**
4. Data Identify three or more sources of information.	**4. Data** *1. Use the Internet.* *2. Look at M. C. Escher's work.* *3. Ask librarian for materials.* *4. Interview eye doctor.*	**4. Data**
5. Time Line Create a three-week time line. Week #1: Gather sources and skim. When information on your questions appears, read it in depth and take notes. Make a reference list.	**5. Time Line** Week #1: *Get librarian materials and my Escher book. Schedule time with eye doctor. Skim Internet and books. Take notes on my two questions. Write interview questions.*	**5. Time Line**

Figure 2.18   Student Project Planning Form

Project Steps	Example	Student
Week #2: Reread notes. If needed, add more information and citations. Gather materials for class presentation. Rewrite notes into meaningful categories. Include ones that answer project questions. Use graphic organizer and rubric to begin paper. Week #3: Draft paper per the rubric and edit. Review rubric. Write final copy and reference list. Self-assess with rubric and turn both in. Organize presentation.	Week #2: *Redo my notes with eye doctor's information. Select visuals for paper and presentation. Make my own visual illusion. Use graphic organizer for paper.* Week #3: *Make handouts for class.* *Outline my presentation and check the project rubric. Draft paper and ask Saul to edit. Write final copy, assess it and turn that in.*	
6. Feedback Give presentation, self-assess with rubric. Ask class for feedback.	**6. Feedback** *Complete rubric after talk. Ask class for their opinions.*	**6. Feedback**

#44: PULLING IT TOGETHER: CLASS BOOKS

Students can take responsibility for their learning by compiling class books. Such books consist of multiple dated entries that chronicle the full range of learning experiences over the duration of a course. Three-ring binders give students the greatest flexibility in developing their books since pages may be added at any time. For example, students can make new entries after homework has been corrected or after they have revised their books' contents based on their semimonthly book discussions with their peers.

There are three documents that may be revised until the end of the course. These include the table of contents, a student-made course time line, and student-made time lines that note their learning milestones at the end of the class. Figure 2.19 below shows a sample table of contents that can be used to construct any class book.

Figure 2.19   Class Book

Table of Contents

Class outlines, syllabi, or other teacher materials

Background knowledge samples

Notes

Assignments

Group work artifacts

Tests

Journals

Sample text selections

Homework

Agendas for class sessions or special events

Goal sheets

Pictures, photos

Contracts

Projects

Course time line and personal milestones

SUGGESTIONS FOR FURTHER INFORMATION ABOUT ACTIVE LEARNING

Campbell, L., Campbell, B., & Dickinson, D. (2004). *Teaching and learning through multiple intelligences* (3rd ed.). Boston: Pearson.

Educators wanting scores of ideas for teaching through multiple modes will find them available in this book. After briefly introducing Gardner's Theory of Multiple Intelligences, the book provides checklists for identifying the eight intelligences, classroom environment and resource considerations, hundreds of instructional and assessment processes, and Web sites for the intelligences. Sample ready-to-use lesson plans and curricular units as well as K–12 classroom and whole-school models are also provided

Moore, R., & Moore, M. (2004). *Active teaching and learning strategies: Creating a blueprint for success.* Cary, NC: Trafton Publishing.

Academic standards and student data are the starting points for this book's classroom practices. Written by educational administrators, the Moores promote a four-part instructional design that consists of academic, social, contextual, and developmental student needs. These four components are addressed through the use of active learning strategies. The authors maintain that the difference between effective and outstanding teachers is that outstanding teachers care about their students, use data effectively, teach with active techniques, and insure that their students become active learners themselves.

Web Sites on Experiential Learning. Available at www.njaes.rutgers.edu/learnbydoing/weblinks.html

This Web site provides six pages of links to experiential learning-by-doing resources. The content is divided into the helpful categories of journal articles, reviews, background information, organizations, and resource materials. There is likely something for nearly everyone on this site. Some of the topics featured include theories of experiential education, strategies for its application in diverse subject areas, using hands-on learning with young children to adults, and organizations to contact for more information.

Willis, J. (2006). *Research-based strategies to ignite student learning.* Alexandria, VA: Association for Supervision and Curriculum Development.

Drawing on her neurological expertise and classroom experience, the author, a board-certified neurologist and middle school teacher, examined decades of learning-centered brain research to determine what information was most valid and relevant for educators. The result is a comprehensive and accessible guide for improving student learning based on substantial academic research.

3

Ensuring Gender-Fair Instruction

Gender concerns in education originally focused on the needs of girls. During the 80s and 90s, complaints were raised about girls' experiences in schools and out. Girls were portrayed as invisible in the curriculum and shortchanged in classroom discussions and on the playground. They lagged behind boys in math and science, were overlooked by teachers, and suffered from low self-esteem and, later, economic inequities (American Association of University Women Educational Foundation, 1992; Sadker & Sadker, 1994).

By 2007, girls had virtually closed the math and science gap (National Assessment of Educational Progress, 2007). They take more Advanced Placement (AP) classes, maintain their lead in reading and writing, and graduate from high school, enroll in college, and earn diplomas at higher rates than their male peers (Greene & Winters, 2006; Mead, 2006; U.S. Department of Education, 2004). Economically, however, young women struggle to catch up to the wages that men earn.

The college degrees women earn prepare them for low-paying occupations such as teaching. In addition, degreed women in their mid-twenties to thirties rarely earn more than their male cohorts who attended but never completed college. Even after controlling for professional choices, recent female college graduates earn less than men. These statistics only recount the beginning of the female work experience.

While K–12 gains among female students have been applauded, concerns have been voiced since the 90s that boys trail girls academically. NAEP test score and high school graduation data show that boys have lower grades and test scores than girls, are labeled with learning disabilities and medicated more often, behaviorally act out and drop out in larger numbers, and enroll in college in smaller numbers (Coley, 2001; Educational Research Service, 2007a; Greene & Winters, 2006; Gurian, Henley, & Trueman, 2001; Sadker & Sadker, 2001; Sommers, 2000; Viadero, 2006).

To clarify some of the statistical gender differences in educational outcomes, Tables 3.1A and 3.1B are provided below. They address limited aspects of high school student data. This includes scores of the 2005 National Assessment of Educational Progress for reading and writing across Grades 4, 8, and 12.

High school graduation data are also listed but the data source warrants explanation. As readers likely know, states use varying methods to calculate the number of their student graduates. Without a standardized approach, there is a significant range in such data, and debates flourish about what constitutes accurate reporting methods (Greene & Winters, 2002, 2006; Mishel, 2006; National Governors Association, 2005). The tables below rely on the work of the Manhattan Institute's Jay Greene and Marcus Winters. These analysts disagree with "official" governmental approaches and devised their own independent, respected method for determining graduate numbers. Since their data is retrieved from the National Center for Education Statistic's Common Core of Data (CCD), the results below are for 2003. This year, rather than a more recent one, was necessitated by the length of time it takes CCD to make its information available. Even though the data may not be current, graduation rates do not vary dramatically from year to year (Greene & Winters, 2006). Greene and Winters' method of determining graduation rates varies from others in that it tracks students for four sequential years and does not count GEDs as synonymous with diplomas.

Moving into murky waters, we have included incomplete data on American Indian/Alaska Native students. As 1 percent of the national population, Native students are frequently lumped into an "other" category so that their educational experiences remain unknown and invisible. Because of their unique treaty status, heritage, and role in American society, we think it important to include their graduation rates. Such data are difficult to locate. Fortunately, Greene and Winters determined Native 2002 student graduation rates. The data are included below even though they were analyzed in a study different from the one used for other student groups. Further, there was no disaggregation for gender.

Table 3.1A Percentages of Male Students by Race and Grade Level With at or Above Basic Achievement on 2005 NAEP Scores and 2002 High School Graduation Rates

Males by Race	Math 4th	Math 8th	Math 12th	Rdg 4th	Rdg 8th	Rdg 12th	HS Grad*
White	90	76	69	72	76	69	74
Black	59	43	46	36	43	46	48
Hispanic	69	50	55	42	50	55	49
Asian/Pacific Is.	89	75	70	68	75	70	71
American Indian/Alaska Native	73	57	No data	44	57	No data	57**

SOURCES: National Assessments of Educational Progress, National Public School Students, 2005

* High school graduation rates from Jay Greene and Marcus Winters (2006) of the Manhattan Institute

**Native student high school graduation rates are from Jay Greene and Marcus Winters (2002) of the Manhattan Institute.

Table 3.1B Percentages of Female Students by Race and Grade Level With at or Above Basic Achievement on 2005 NAEP Scores and 2002 High School Graduation Rates

Females by Race	Math 4th	Math 8th	Math 12th	Rdg 4th	Rdg 8th	Rdg 12th	HS Grad*
White	89	86	87	77	86	87	79
Black	69	58	57	46	58	57	59
Hispanic	65	60	63	47	60	63	58
Asian/Pacific Is.	90	83	73	75	83	73	74
American Indian/Alaska Native	66	66	No data	54	66	No data	57**

SOURCES: National Assessments of Educational Progress, National Public School Students, 2005

* High school graduation rates from Jay Greene and Marcus Winters (2006) of the Manhattan Institute

**Native student high school graduation rates are from Jay Greene and Marcus Winters (2002) of the Manhattan Institute.

Some striking conclusions can be drawn from the data above. First, it is clear girls typically outperform boys at all grade levels in math and reading. They also surpass their counterparts in graduating, which raises the important question about why fewer males earn diplomas. Though such information is not included above, it is interesting and saddening to note that other nations grapple with similar problems of male student underachievement. Australia, Canada, the United Kingdom and other countries are actively seeking ways to increase boys' achievement (Bishop, 2006; Educational Research Service, 2007a).

Another disturbing conclusion in the above data is the wide disparity between white and minority students. Many researchers assert that such test results highlight the deep-seated problems of race and class in the United States (Barnett & Rivers, 2006; Educational Research Service, 2007a; Mead, 2006). Racial and economic inequities continue to extract their toll on student achievement.

Though not included here, it is interesting to point out that there is some good news about NAEP's long-term trend data. Long-term NAEP scores as of 2007 show that fourth and eighth grade boys have improved in reading since 1992. In fact, as of 2007, all groups of 9- and 13-year-old boys with the exception of Native American boys have improved their reading skills, with tremendous gains among African Americans. Similarly, most boys of all ages and races are scoring significantly better in math. Older males at the 12th grade, however, have declining performances in reading.

Simultaneously, girls are improving at faster rates than anticipated. Girls' scores in math and science have improved so that they have virtually closed the previous gap with boys. They maintain their lead in reading, as they always have since NAEP was first administered in 1971. In writing, girls have dramatically pulled ahead of boys.

However, among this good news, a deeply disturbing fact from the above two tables is that high school graduation rates are alarmingly low for male and female students. Approximately half of our minority students and 30 percent of our mainstream students do not graduate from high school. The greatest gender disparity is among African American females and males.

It is problematic to assume that low graduation rates are simply a high school concern. Some researchers, such as Robert Balfanz and Nettie Legters of Johns Hopkins University, have identified middle school achievement as an important factor in whether students graduate from high school (Lloyd, 2007). Less prepared students, specifically boys, have greater difficulty making the transition from 8th to 9th grade. Diploma Counts 2007 showed that more than 30 percent of students are lost from high school pipelines, which has been identified as the "largest leak in the education pipeline (Haney et al., 2004). Clearly, we need to adequately prepare students of all grades and of both genders to increase graduation rates.

Causes of Gender Disparity in Education

What causes the varying outcomes of male and female students in K–12 education? A number of theories attempt to explain gender inequities, though the research is inconclusive and direct causal links are difficult to prove. Teachers, however, must still respond to the situation before them. Some insight into the potential causes of gender-based underachievement is better than none since otherwise inappropriate plans and policies could be promoted. Below, we briefly summarize four of the most prominent theories explaining gender inequities in education:

1. Socialization Factors:

   Some researchers assert that the notion of the ideal student is closer to the stereotypic behavior of girls rather than that of boys (Hunsader, 2002; Lingard et al., 2002). Most boys want to be seen as masculine and as a result may hide their interest in academics (Hunsader, 2002; Pollack, 1998). Outside of school, societal influences from families, other adults, student jobs, as well as the media and entertainment industry may reinforce constrictive social roles. (American Association of University Women [AAUW] Educational Foundation, 1998; Brown & Gilligan, 1992; Educational Research Service, 2007a; Gilligan, 1982; James, 2007; Kindlon & Thompson, 1999; Sadker & Sadker, 1994).

2. Educational Factors:

   School curricula, teaching methods, and differential treatment by teachers may affect girls and boys differently (AAUW, 1998; Sadker & Sadker, 2001). As NAEP test scores show, boys have historically trailed girls in reading. Varying the types of reading, materials, structuring writing in stages and providing boys with real-world audiences can spark interest and achievement. Some researchers also recommend providing active and less active choices for assignments to meet the needs of both male and female students (Gurian & Stevens, 2005; James, 2007; Kindlon & Thompson, 1999). Visual tasks as well as competitive and technology-oriented ones can also prove beneficial.

3. Lack of Role Models, Mentors, and Social Networks

There are limited role models in school and out for both male and female students. (Brown & Gilligan, 1992; Educational Research Service, 2004, 2007a; Education Review Office, 2000; James, 2007; Kindlon & Thompson, 1999; PBS, 2007). While teachers are primarily female, they can serve as positive role models for girls but not necessarily for boys. However, schools do not have ready access to those in other professions who could inspire both genders. Additionally, many boys lack fathers, and, when they are present, they may show more interest in their sons' sports activities than in academics. Often boys and girls feel isolated and school and lack networks that reinforce academic goals.

4. Biological Factors

A hotly contested theory is that boys and girls are hardwired differently and such biological factors influence behavior and learning. Girls may have verbal advantages neurologically while boys tend to perform better on visual-spatial tasks (Gurian & Stevens, 2005; Kimura, 2002). Girls may multitask more easily while boys may compartmentalize brain activity, which could indicate a preference for focusing on a single task for an extended period of time (Gurian & Stevens, 2005). Girls' prefrontal cortex develops faster, which may suggest better impulse control (Neu & Weinfeld, 2007). Boys may require movement and action to learn (Gurian & Stevens, 2005; Hunsader, 2002; James, 2007). Other researchers contend that the two genders are more alike than different biologically (Campbell & Sanders, 2002; Kafer, 2007; Sylwester, 2005). Further, they contend that there is greater variation among individuals of the same sex than across the genders. Lastly, it is also interesting to note that research from the first round of MRI studies of normal child brain development conducted by the National Institutes of Health found less gender-related variation than previous studies and that any that existed disappeared by adolescence (Children's' Hospital Boston, 2007).

WHAT DO RESEARCH STUDIES SHOW ABOUT GENDER-EQUITABLE APPROACHES TO IMPROVING STUDENT ACHIEVEMENT?

While the debate about the causes of disproportionate achievement among males and females continues, many studies suggest that school and classroom-based efforts can improve student learning.

First, those of us who teach can reflect on the dynamics in our classrooms. Few of us have received much training or inservice professional development on gender equity issues. Since it is estimated that teachers have up to 1,000 interactions with students in a single day (Bullock, 1997), there is ample opportunity for behavior to speak more loudly than words. Teacher observations, whether of ourselves on video or as feedback from colleagues, have been shown to heighten our awareness of our practices as well as the different needs of our students (AAUW, 1998; Bullock, 1997; Campbell & Sanders, 1997; Educational Research Service, 2007a; Teachers 21, 2007).

A second reflective approach to reducing gender disparity is to take stock of our classroom materials and visuals. For example, studies suggest that students spend as much as 80 percent to 95 percent of their time using textbooks, and that many instructional decisions are based on textbooks (Hulme, 1988; Woodward & Elliot, 1990). Though progress has been made in developing nonsexist materials, they nevertheless are not bias free. For example, in language arts, math, social studies, and science, more males than females are often represented in the text and illustrations, the worldviews and perspectives of minority groups and women are often limited, and many posters and displays do not show men valuing learning or women in nontraditional fields (Educational Development Corporation, 1999; National Council of Teachers of English, 2002; Sadker & Sadker, 1994; Teachers21, 2007; Wilson, 2003). This underrepresentation communicates that women as a group are less important in society and that education is irrelevant in the adult lives of men. By knowing what to look for, teachers can assess the texts and other classroom materials to identify inequities, supplement them as appropriate, or use them as examples of a biased perspective. In this chapter, we suggest strategies for doing so.

Reflective approaches are not enough, however, to create equitable learning environments. Attention must be given to improving the reading and writing skills of boys since they have lagged behind girls in these skills for at least 30 years according to NAEP data. At the same time, researchers have noted that many girls like "boy-friendly" strategies and that ultimately all students are individuals and benefit from a wide range of learning options (Educational Research Service, 2007a; Neu & Weinfeld, 2007; Newkirk, 2002). For example, both male and female students value a wider array of reading materials in the classroom. Yet, when teachers include magazines, nonfiction, humorous texts, Web sites, and graphic oriented materials, boys engage more actively with reading and see it connected to their out-of-school literacies (Kommer, 2006; Munns et al., 2006; Newkirk, 2002). Similarly, movement and manipulatives can improve reading (Devon County Council [UK], 2000; Education Review Office, 2000; James, 2007).

Increasing the writing achievement of boys has been researched as well. A 2003 study conducted by the U.K. Office for Standards in Education revealed several effective strategies. These included having students write frequently and at length to develop stamina and familiarity with writing processes. Students are seldom asked to rewrite longer pieces unless it is for publication. While the genre or form can be teacher prescribed, students choose the content, work on it in stages, and receive frequent, prompt feedback. Teachers also show that they value different styles of writing including boys' succinctness and logical thought, as well as humor and the writing they do outside of school humor

(Fletcher, 2006). To improve girls' achievement, encourage them to write about their understanding of concepts since girls are often comfortable and excel at doing so.

Mentoring and support programs, whether formal or informal, established by one classroom teacher or a schoolwide effort, can translate into reduced absenteeism, stronger achievement and graduation rates for both male and female students (Corbett & Wilson, 2000; Educational Research Service, 2007a; James, 2007; Taylor & Lorimer, 2003; Younger & Warrington, 2005; Zirkel, 2002). In fact, in one longitudinal study, Zirkel found that students who had at least one race and gender-based role model performed better academically at least two years after the mentoring had occurred. The effects did not end there. Students also reported that they thought more about their futures than did those who did not have matched mentors. Additional studies show that students, school staff, community members, and family members can all provide the needed encouragement, connectedness, and support to help students of both genders improve academically, transition from middle school successfully, and graduate with a diploma. As Younger & Warrington (2005) suggest, students involved in supportive relationships may in turn influence many of their peers who did not directly participate in such processes. Research has demonstrated additional ways to increase the academic success of boys or girls, or both genders simultaneously. Several of these strategies are featured in this chapter. One important example of such techniques is implementing transition programs from middle school to high school (Cooney & Bottoms, 2002; Educational Research Service, 2004; Letrello & Miles, 2003; Southern Regional Education Board, 2002). Others include using competitive learning approaches on occasion (Devon County Council [UK], 2000; Goldstein, Haldane, & Mitchell, 1990; James, 2007; Noble & Bradford, 2000); cooperative learning that taps girls' skills at seeking consensus and building on others' ideas; asking all students higher-level questions in discussions and in writing; providing hands-on and kinesthetic activities; using short, chunked, time-limited tasks; and giving clear, specific instructions (AAUW, 1998; Noble & Bradford, 2000; James, 2007; PBS Parents, 2007; Slavin, 1990) . Continued work remains necessary to increase female students' interest in computer science so that they are better prepared for future profitable career opportunities (National Center for Education Statistics, 2005b). As it stands currently, female participation in advanced computer science classes during high school and in college are both at 15 percent.

While gender issues continue to influence the education of all students, teachers can make enormous differences in their classrooms for both female and male students. This chapter supports such efforts with four types of techniques: teacher self-reflection, assessment of gender issues in classroom materials, gender-fair instruction, and considering transition programs to increase high school graduation rates. Ultimately, all educators know that the way each student learns is highly idiosyncratic. As teachers, we can become adept observers of our students and accommodate them for the individuals they are.

#45: CONDUCTING A CLASSROOM GENDER AUDIT

Gender concerns exist, in part, because society has historically perceived and subsequently treated girls and boys differently. The first step in promoting equity in the classroom is to become aware of potential gender-based classroom dynamics and work toward changing them. The classroom audit in Figure 3.1 below can be scored individually or by a colleague.

Figure 3.1 Teacher Rating on Gender Issues

Equity Issue	Often	Sometimes	Could Improve
Environmental Considerations			
1. Males and females are equally represented in bulletin boards, posters, and wall decorations.			
2. Classroom visuals portray males in nurturing roles.			
3. Classroom visuals portray females in active roles.			
4. Work samples of girls and boys are displayed equally.			
5. Books in the classroom library feature females and males in nontraditional roles.			
Teacher Behaviors			
6. Gender-fair language is used. Exclusive *she* or *he* references to roles such as nurses or mechanics are avoided.			
7. Wait time of 5 to 10 seconds is provided after asking a question.			
8. Language, voice, tone, and nonverbals are monitored for sexist generalizations.			
9. The same amount and type of casual conversation occurs with male and female students.			
10. Teacher requests for help are equitably assigned to female and male students.			
11. Girls and boys are called on equally in class.			
12. Classroom disrupters receive similar responses from the teacher.			
13. Boys and girls are seated in the classroom according to relevant rationales.			
Instructional Strategies			
14. Higher-level questions are alternated between male and female students.			
15. Active, hands-on learning is provided to all students.			
16. Classwork is accomplished in cross-gender groupings.			
17. Curricular materials feature both genders in a wide variety of roles.			
18. Female and male role models are highlighted in course materials and classroom guests.			
19. Specific, constructive feedback is offered to all students.			

#46: SEEKING STUDENT FEEDBACK ON GENDER DYNAMICS

Figure 3.2 was developed for teachers who are interested in learning students' perceptions of gender dynamics in the classroom.

Figure 3.2 Student Perspectives of Gender Dynamics in the Classroom

Teacher's Name: _____

Class Name: _____ Date: _____

I am a (check one): _____ Female student _____ Male student

Please check the response that fits you the best:	Never	Sometimes	Often
The Classroom Environment			
1. Pictures on the walls show boys and girls equally.			
2. Both boys' and girls' work is posted for everyone to see.			
3. There are an equal number of books and other reading materials for boys and girls.			
4. I feel welcome in this class.			
5. I feel invisible or unappreciated in this class.			
6. The teacher talks to me as much as to others in the class.			
7. The teacher expects me to do my best in this class.			
8. The teacher expects all others to do their best in this class.			
Teaching and Learning Experiences			
9. We learn from teacher lectures.			
10. We learn through whole-class discussions.			
11. We learn through hands-on activities.			
12. We learn cooperatively in small groups.			
13. We learn by working alone.			
14. The teacher calls on girls to respond to questions.			
15. The teacher calls on boys to respond to questions.			
16. I am interrupted when I speak in class.			
17. The teacher gives me enough time to respond to questions.			
18. The teacher is fair with me if I misbehave.			
19. The teacher is fair with others if they misbehave.			
20. The teacher helps all of us with assignments equally.			

My favorite way to learn is _____

One thing I would change to make the class better for girls is _____

_____

One thing I would change to make this class better for boys is _____

_____

One thing I would change to make this class better for me is _____

_____

#47: ASSESSING BIAS
IN CURRICULAR MATERIALS

For teachers to detect potential bias in instructional materials, it is helpful to recognize the different ways it can manifest. Sadker & Sadker (2001) identified seven types of bias that often appear in educational materials. Figure 3.3 adapts the Sadkers' work to serve as a tool for assessing whether gender limitations are evident in classroom materials.

Figure 3.3 Rating Gender Bias in Instructional Materials

Title of instructional resource: _____

Form of Bias	No Bias Evident	Bias Evident	Ways to Reduce Bias
Omission—males and females are not equally featured in text and illustrations			
Sexist Language—masculine pronouns and terms such as *mankind* and *forefathers* are used			
Stereotyping—the genders are portrayed in "traditional" roles, such as male heavy-equipment operators and female nurses			
Imbalance—minimal information is given on important issues, e.g., one paragraph explains the suffrage movement in the United States			
Unreality—controversial topics are ignored in favor of traditional views, e.g., avoidance of divorce statistics when describing families			
Fragmentation—groups are portrayed in a fragmented or clustered fashion so that all women writers are featured together rather than integrated throughout			
Cosmetic Bias—efforts are made to have materials look balanced when only minimal coverage is actually offered			

SOURCE: From David Sadker & Myra Sadker. (2001). In James Banks (Ed.), *Multicultural Education: Issues and Perspectives* (4th ed.). Published by John Wiley & Sons. Adapted with permission of the publisher.

#48: QUALITY QUESTIONING

The questions teachers or others ask place different cognitive demands on students. All students should be asked to respond to higher-level questions regardless of gender or other perceptions of abilities. The following questions can be photocopied and cut into strips for easy referencing during class discussions. If desired, students can use them in small-group formats. A word of caution: wait five seconds before asking a student to respond to one of these questions to increase the quality of thinking. Please note, other questioning strategies that you may also consider using are Strategies #11, #12 and #34.

Questions for Critical Thinking

What examples can you give?

What alternatives might exist?

What questions do you have?

What steps can we take to . . . ?

What information do we need to decide?

What conclusion can you draw?

What is an explanation for . . . ?

Do you agree with . . . ? Why? How do you know?

What choice would you have made?

What might happen if . . . ?

What evidence supports . . . ?

What is a likely outcome? Why?

What are the advantages or disadvantages of . . . ?

Whose point of view is evident?

Is this information bias-free?

What are some unstated assumptions?

What is the theme or message?

Questions for Evaluative Thinking

What is your opinion of . . . ? Why?

Why did he or she choose to . . . ?

What was most or least effective?

What would you recommend?

What standards could we develop to assess . . . ?

What criteria would you use to determine . . . ?

How well does this meet the goals?

How would you prove or disprove . . . ?

How do we know this evidence is reliable?

What evidence exists . . . for . . . ?

What is the importance of . . . ?

What is your conclusion?

Would it be better if . . . ?

What choice would you have made?

Who might disagree with you and why?

What advantages and disadvantages exist?

How do the results compare to the criteria?

Were the requirements met?

What value does this have?

#49: USING INCLUSIVE LANGUAGE

Nonsexist language is referred to as gender-neutral or inclusive language. It treats females and males equitably. Because English has no generic singular, in the past he, his, and him were commonly used in expressions such as the student . . . he. Suggestions for using inclusive language follow; they make simple changes to personal pronouns and commonly used, everyday nouns.

Personal Pronouns

1. Reword in plural form.

Examples	*Replacements*
He must turn in his assignment.	Students should turn in their assignments.
The counselor will schedule his own appointment.	The counselors will schedule their appointments.

2. Eliminate gender references.

Examples	*Replacements*
No one should leave her car unlocked.	Cars should be locked.
He must return it by that date.	It must be returned by that date.

3. Alternate female and male references (sparingly).

Examples	*Replacements*
Encourage each child to attend as she is able.	Encourage each child to attend as he is able.
Has he been able to do so?	Has she been able to do so?
Did he contribute?	Did she contribute?

Figure 3.4 Using Inclusive Language

Nouns: Students might go on a word search to add to this list.

Instead of:	*Use:*
actress	actor
brotherhood	human family
businessman	businessperson
chairman	chairperson
coed	student
cleaning lady	housekeeper, janitor
congressman	member of congress, representative
fireman	firefighter
founding fathers	founding leaders
housewife	homemaker
mailman	postal worker, mail deliverer
manhood	adulthood
mankind	humanity
manmade	synthetic, handmade
manpower	personnel, staff
middleman	go-between, intermediary
newsman	reporter
policeman	police officer
repairman	technician, mechanic, electrician
salesman	salesperson
sisterhood	human family
spokesman	spokesperson
sportsman	athlete
stewardess	flight attendant
watchman	security guard
workman	worker

#50: THINKING WHILE LISTENING

Boys and girls approach learning from somewhat different perspectives and with slightly different needs. Many girls tend to use a conversational style, share ideas that build on one another, and seek consensus. Cooperative learning complements these inherent strengths while also tapping the interests of peer-based learning among boys. Thinking While Listening is particularly effective for use with worksheets and while practicing skills.

1. Identify a collaborative skill students should practice. Sample skills include using appropriate behavior, staying on task, paraphrasing or summarizing, using effective listening skills, or critiquing ideas appropriately.

2. Divide students into small groups of about four. You may want to have students count off in numbers from one to four and cluster ones, twos, threes, and fours together respectively.

3. Provide each group with a worksheet or assignment.

4. Select one problem from the assignment. Model thinking through the problem out loud, with students observing your efforts. Ask students for feedback on your thinking process, on whether your response was accurate and effective, and why or why not. Be sure that all students understand the procedures they are to use.

5. Instruct the group members to divide the problems equally among themselves. Also remind them of the collaborative skill they are practicing.

6. Each student takes a turn solving a problem. Group members concurrently encourage and evaluate one another's efforts.

7. After all group members take their turns, give the groups time to determine that every member understands all the problems. Also, have them reflect on how effectively they use the collaborative skill.

8. If desired, give students a new assignment sheet with similar problems. Have them complete the second assignment individually as an accountability measure.

#51: MIX AND MATCH

The cooperative learning activity below assists students in developing expertise and teaching one another. It can be used with teacher-made information cards, with sections of an assigned chapter, or with entire chapters or books. It is based on the jigsaw technique originally developed by Aronson, Stephan, Sikes, Blaney, and Snapp (1978).

1. Organize materials into four sections, numbering each section, 1, 2, 3, and 4.

2. Cluster students into groups of four. Provide each group with the complete set of instructional materials divided into fourths. Explain that students must teach their peers about the content they each have received. Note, these groups are referred to as the master group.

3. To teach their groups, students must first learn their content. They do so by working with those who have the same information. Organize students so that all the ones are together in a group, all the twos are together in another, and so on. (See Figure 3.5.)

4. The expert groups develop strategies to teach their content.

5. The experts return to the master groups and teach the content.

Figure 3.5 Master and Expert Groupings

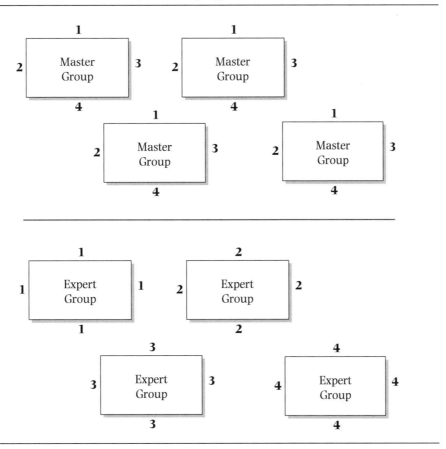

52: PLAYING GAMES

Many students enjoy classroom challenges and games. Two simple games are provided below. The first, called Flash Card Tag, can be used for any type of classroom content available on flash cards such as math, geographic facts, or spelling words. The second game, called Fast Tracking (Multiplication in this case) asks students to practice multiplication facts but other number games could easily be substituted.

Flash Card Tag

Step 1: Place two identical sets of flash cards on two desks in the front of the room.

Step 2: Divide students into two groups of single-file lines facing forward. The first student from each team should be about 10 feet from the desk with the flash cards.

Step 3: Use a signal to begin play. The first student goes to the desk, takes the first flash card, holds it up, announces the answer to the class, places the card in a discard pile, and then tags the next person in line.

Step 4: If students do not know the answer or give an incorrect one, they must put the card on the bottom of the pile and select the next card. They will continue to select cards until they get a correct answer or until they have drawn four cards.

Step 5: The first team to correctly give the answer to all the flash cards wins.

Fast Tracking Multiplication Or . . .

This competitive game is adapted from the simple card game called War. It requires a deck of cards for every two players in the room. Before the game begins, write on an overhead that Ace = 1, J = 10, Q = 11, K = 12. The steps follow:

Step 1: Organize students into pairs. Give each pair a deck of cards. Tell them to shuffle the deck.

Step 2: The pairs divide their cards evenly, stacking the cards face down on their desks.

Step 3: Each member of the pair turns over the top card at the same time. They multiply the two cards and shout out the answer. Students who call out the correct answer first add their teammate's cards to their pile. If a tie occurs, the pairs continue to turn over their cards until someone wins the pile.

When the original stack of cards has been played through, the pairs count their winnings. Whoever has the most cards wins a pencil, a point, or a round of applause. If another round of play is desired, partners can be switched.

#53: SEQUENCE CARDS

Many students, females and males alike, enjoy opportunities to physically engage with their learning, whether through touch or movement. Using sequence cards is a simple way to add tactile and kinesthetic components to learning.

Sequence cards are sets of four-by-six-inch notecards featuring a succession of words, numbers, events, steps, or other sequences. Sets of cards might include the parts of a sentence, numbers and symbols in a mathematical formula, historical events in chronological order, words or letters in alphabetical order, or steps in a process such as how a bill becomes law (see Figure 3.6). Hand out the cards randomly to students with the directions that all students who get a card go to the front of the class and put themselves in the proper order.

Figure 3.6 Sets of Sequence Cards

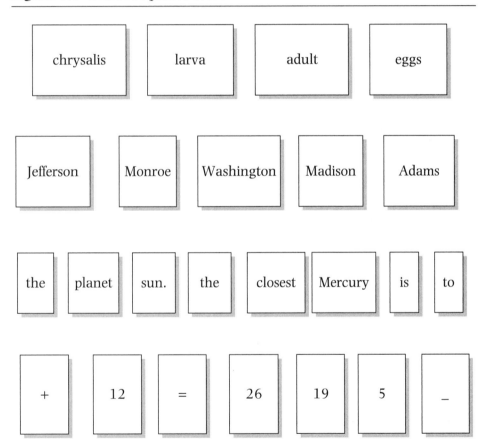

#54: PAPER PLATE REVIEW

This strategy engages students physically in recalling facts or concepts. The needed supplies are minimal: paper plates, marking pens, a paper clip, and information from a recent unit of study.

To do a paper plate review:

1. Choose 8 to 12 questions, such as those in Figure 3.7, related to a topic of study.

2. Make a spinner. Put each question in one section of the spinner. A paper clip makes a good pointer.

3. Write the answer to each question on four to five paper plates and spread them around the room face up.

4. One student spins and calls out the questions, while the remaining students touch a plate with the correct answer with a finger or foot.

5. Two rules are necessary. Students cannot touch anyone else, and they must be quiet enough to hear the questions.

Figure 3.7 Spinner for Paper Plate Review Game

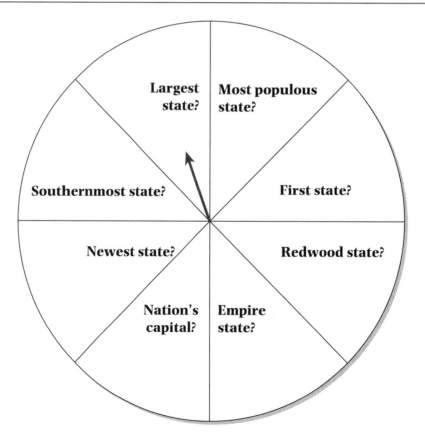

#55: HEADBANDS

Students (especially boys) like this game because they move around the room while trying to guess vocabulary words written on headbands they each wear. Classmates give clues about essential attributes, characteristics, or the qualities of a word or concept's meaning. Note, other vocabulary building strategies are available in #16, #17, #18 and #36.

1. Identify several vocabulary words or concepts that you want to reinforce.

2. Write three guiding questions on the whiteboard. Sample questions are:

   What classification of things does it fit into?

   What are its essential characteristics?

   What are some examples of it?

3. Put one word or concept on a 2-inch by 24-inch strip and make enough strips for the entire class. Staple the strips to make headbands.

4. Distribute headbands, asking the students to put them on without looking at the words, or place the headbands on each student yourself.

5. When all students have their headbands on, they get up and walk around the room asking each other three questions to guess the word. This can also be done in small groups if you have limited space.

6. An example headband might have the word "antibody" from a science unit. Responses could be "substances to fight diseases," "antitoxins," or "the big police force of the body."

7. Give students enough time so most can guess their words. Then have them remove their headbands to check if their guesses were correct.

It is often a good idea to put the most difficult words on the heads of your students with the most challenges because it is the other students who will be giving the clues.

#56: A WORD TOOL KIT

Poor literacy impedes academic success and is a problem that confronts far too many boys (and girls, and adults for that matter!). A Word Tool Kit below teaches students word attack skills, skills that are sorely needed among those who struggle with reading. Once again, prior vocabulary activities are available in strategies #16, #17, #18, #36, and #55.

Figure 3.8   A Word Tool Kit

A Word Tool Kit

When you see a word you don't know, use the following word tools:

1. Sound it out.
2. Break the word into syllables.
3. Look for smaller words or word parts that you recognize.
4. Keep reading to see what makes sense.
5. Use the words around it to identify the meaning.
6. Think of a different word that makes sense.
7. Ask your partner.
8. Use a dictionary.
9. Guess and go on.
10. Ask your teacher.
11. Use picture clues.
12. Use the sounds of the first letters to get you going.
13. Add suffixes.
14. Consider whether you have seen the word before and what it meant then.

#57: BITE-SIZE READING

When students read textbooks, they encounter many tasks simultaneously. They find new words and information, key concepts, and supporting details, and they juggle these and other tasks in an effort to comprehend their reading assignments. The complexity of reading new content can become more manageable with bite-size pieces, especially for male students who struggle with reading and sometimes prefer chunked approaches to learning new content. The following encourages students to interact with content in small amounts and then go back for more.

Step 1: Assign students to read silently for 15 minutes.

Step 2: Pair students up for 5 minutes to discuss what they just read. Sometimes it helps to ask the pair to make at least five notes.

Step 3: Teacher leads a whole-class discussion on the main ideas and supporting details for 3 to 5 minutes.

Step 4: Students read silently for 10 to 15 minutes, and the process repeats itself.

This strategy can be adapted to include a visual component. Ask students to read short sections of text and then create visual symbols of what they read. Students can work in teams to translate their new knowledge into visual representations.

#58: TEACHING BOYS TO WRITE

Thanks to literacy researchers, much has been learned recently about how to improve boys' writing skills. The following list compiles a variety of ways to tap boys' strengths while nurturing better literacy skills.

1. Encourage brief whole-class, small-group, or paired discussion before boys start a writing assignment. This taps their oral skills and allows them to talk to learn.

2. Allow students to draw, or use visual graphic organizers, to organize their thoughts before writing. At times, encourage the inclusion of drawings or sketches in text.

3. Give clear directions about what you want. For example, instead of saying "Explain" ask for three or more details.

4. Frequently give choice as to the content, not necessarily the genre, of writing so that boys can select topics of interest to them.

5. Tackle writing projects in stages with feedback at each stage of planning and drafting.

6. Encourage a diversity of style, such as succinctness, humor, and logical thought.

7. Give prompt, detailed feedback. Acknowledge and share small and large successes.

8. Have a variety of audiences and outside-of-school purposes for the writing.

9. Avoid asking that all writing be rewritten. Ask students to revise their best pieces of work.

10. Find out what kinds of writing boys do outside of school and bring some of that into the classroom.

11. Have students write frequently and for multiple purposes.

12. Instead of assigning a journal, use something more appealing, such as a notebook or class lab text that includes quotes, facts, cartoons, or drawings.

13. Don't assign writing for punishment, since that creates negative associations.

14. See if some boys want to form an informal writing group.

#59: SIX TIPS FOR TECH-SAVVY GIRLS

Even though girls and boys have equal access to computers at school and at home, they do not leave high school with equal amounts of technology knowledge. Girls constitute less than 15 percent of the students enrolled in advanced computer science courses as of 2006 (National Center for Educational Statistics, 2007; National Center for Women and Information Technology, 2007) Research also shows that undergraduate computer science degrees for women have actually decreased by 70 percent between 2000 and 2005 (Cohen, 2005; National Center for Women and Information Technology, 2007). While discouraging, these trends are not the final word. The following strategies have been gathered by the National Center for Women and Technology after surveying 100 successful IT programs. The six tips below can promote girls' interest, retention, and achievement in technology

> **Tip #1:** Present computers as a tool for creating, designing, and communicating, rather than as a machine to be programmed. Provide open-ended project opportunities where girls are responsible for designing games that appeal to other girls.

> **Tip #2:** Incorporate technology into numerous forms of course work, and use a variety of software, including graphics, writing, and art programs. Also allow a few minutes at the beginning or end of class sessions for girls to "play around" with technology.

> **Tip #3:** In the classroom or computer lab, schedule some girls' only computer time. This encourages girls to learn and experiment in a supportive environment with one another.

> **Tip #4:** Invite girls to form a committee to address technology inequities in the school or to do a community service project that requires the use of technology. In such roles, girls become the experts and receive positive feedback for their technology-related skills

> **Tip #5:** Showcase career opportunities. Arrange field trips, schedule a day at an engineering or technology firm or bring in guest speakers who can serve as positive role models for girls.

> **Tip #6:** Establish mentoring relationships with IT professionals. This can be accomplished with a short-term e-mentoring exchange.

#60: CREATING A "BOY-FRIENDLY" CLASSROOM

The following 10 teaching practices tap learning strengths of many boys and girls in the process. They can be implemented—today!

Figure 3.9   A Top Ten List

A Top Ten List
1. Sit boys in the center and front of the classroom.
2. Move around and be active during instruction. Vary your voice.
3. Give instructions in a bulleted list. Be clear and direct.
4. Occasionally allow students to stand and take notes or maybe even toss a ball lightly during a class discussion.
5. Provide hands-on activities including work with computers.
6. Assign work in small chunks and keep it time-limited.
7. Before class discussions or writing assignments, ask students to jot down a quick list of ideas.
8. Assign work with a real purpose or audience.
9. Include challenge, competition, and cooperation at times.
10. Have a period of review or reflection at the end of a lesson.

#61: EXPLORING NEW ROLES AT SCHOOL

Female and male students can pursue new experiences at school to avoid unnecessary constraints on their development as human beings. The suggestions below move students beyond stereotypic roles and experiences. Additionally, mentoring has been shown to have long-lasting positive academic effects.

Tutoring Younger Students

Older students can tutor younger students. In some cases, "near peer" relationships foster greater achievement than adult role models, due to the powerful support community that develops among students.

Girl Examples	*Boy Examples*
Once girls learn word processing, graphics, Internet use, and multimedia production, they can teach similar skills to younger students.	Older boys who are successful readers and writers can tutor younger students who struggle.

Increasing Participation in the Curriculum

Both female and male students can be encouraged to participate in nongender-specific ways at school. Some research has shown that simple invitations to participate will often encourage students to follow through.

Girl Examples	*Boy Examples*
Girls can participate in the trio of core science classes: physics, biology, and chemistry, as well as in algebra, geometry, calculus, advanced computer science, athletics, and extracurricular activities in nontraditional areas.	Boys can participate in school governance, computer buddy programs, peer mediation, conflict resolution, the arts, leadership, and newspaper and journalism classes to improve their reading and writing skills.
Girls also benefit from leadership programs and participation in advanced placement courses.	Boys also benefit from groupings that are stigma-free for basic-skills instruction.

Receiving Mentoring From Positive Role Models

Role modeling is central to learning. Students learn less from what adults say and more by what we do. It's important for all students to see women doing math and science and men involved in writing and care taking.

Girl Examples	*Boy Examples*
Girls can learn about nontraditional career choices from women engineers, mechanics, computer programmers, and economists, as well as learn about coping skills, healthy lifestyles, and personal finance.	Community members can stress the importance of good work and study skills, health, anger management, and career options in writing, the arts, or education.

#62: PEER SUPPORT NETWORKS

Peer support networks are structured approaches to increasing academic achievement, retention, and high school graduation in part through fostering positive relationships and a sense of connectedness and belonging. The networks can be coed or same sex and are led by teachers or community volunteers. The steps for creating such networks follow.

1. Identify a teacher or community member to oversee a peer network. Also identify a group of students who agree to participate in the network by meeting once weekly and calling their partners three times a week for one month.

2. At the first session, ask students to list what they consider to be their academic and social strengths on sheets of paper that are to be distributed as resources to other network members. Any student can freely call any other member of the network for assistance.

3. Also during the first session, ask students to identify academic or social challenges they would like to address. The challenges are turned in to the network leader.

4. Before the next meeting, the network leader reviews the students' challenges and creates pairs to work together for the next month. Ideally, each student has both a strength and challenge to engage during the upcoming month.

5. At the second session, the network leader announces pairs of students to work together. Plans are also made to meet as a group once weekly before or after school or during lunch. The students must also call their partners three times weekly for a month.

6. Partners are responsible for making lists of the assignments and social efforts they undertake as a pair. During their phone calls, they troubleshoot problems and determine whether positive strides are being made.

7. At the weekly meetings, the networkers discuss and refine their support systems.

8. At the end of the month, any individual progress should be specified, ongoing efforts identified, and the contributions made by all participants acknowledged. Most networks work best on a short-term basis. For that reason, it is good to close the network formally after one month.

#63: ORIENTING EIGHTH AND NINTH GRADERS TO HIGH SCHOOL

The following strategies are selected from research-based effective practices for transitioning both male and female students from middle to high school. These practices include orientation activities before middle schoolers leave for high school as well as high school processes that create a sense of belonging and success. The literature also shows that all three groups—students, their parents, and teachers—must be involved in transition efforts for the programs to have a strong academic impact (Cooney & Bottoms, 2002; Educational Research Services, 2004). It may be interesting for teachers to check off what is currently in place at your middle school or high school, and what might be added.

Orienting Strategies Before Middle School Students Enter High School

- High school staff and students do presentations at the middle school.
- Middle school students visit or tour the high school.
- Parents attend orientations and visit the high school. They receive clear information on course choices and academic options.
- Newsletters and announcements are sent to parents from the high school explaining what their children can expect in the transitioning process.
- Field days or fairs are held at the high school to introduce middle schoolers to extracurricular activities.
- Middle school and high school teachers work in teams and across grades to articulate their curricula and to ensure that all students are known and their needs are met.
- High school teachers and students provide middle school students with "shadow" opportunities.
- Middle school students and their parents are invited to attend special high school events.

Once Ninth Graders Enter High School

- Ninth graders are encouraged to sign up for one or more extracurricular activities when they enter the high school.
- A "buddy" system is in place that pairs the ninth graders with older high
- school students for the first month of school.
- Peer ambassador and mentor programs are in place for additional forms of academic and social support.
- Special events are held to welcome the new students.
- Parents are informed of assignments and grades and are asked to help with special events.

64: MIDDLE SCHOOL ACADEMIC PREPARATION FOR HIGH SCHOOL SUCCESS

In addition to addressing the transition needs of students as they shift from one school to the next, it is important that middle schools academically prepare their students for high school success. With the academic struggles that many ninth graders face, the following are essential curricular experiences (Cooney & Bottoms, 2002; Educational Research Service 2004).

- Students study algebra in the middle grades.
- Eighth graders read a large number of books.
- Middle schoolers create curricular plans to enroll in college.
- Students are linked with an adult or peer mentor who is committed to academics.
- Reading instruction is provided.
- Extra help and extra time provided for struggling students through double sessions of academic courses or tutoring;
- The school curriculum provides opportunities for students to participate in college preparatory learning experiences: work with a partner or group to experience integrated learning, such as using mathematical skills in other classes, and hands-on learning such as science experiments and laboratories.

#65: GENDER EQUITY BOOKMARK

Figure 3.10A Bookmark for Easy Referencing in the Classroom

Figure 3.10A   Gender Equity Bookmark

1. Discuss equity issues with students. Ask them to think critically to find gender bias at school and beyond.

2. In the classroom, display positive images of both genders in a variety of roles.

3. Supplement curricular resources as needed to achieve gender equity.

4. Arrange class seating charts to mix genders and, as the teacher, move about the room to be accessible to all.

5. Identify sexist language and replace it with alternate terms.

6. Be a role model of participation in a variety of activities. For example, if you are a male teacher, talk about sewing or cooking; or, if female, talk about working with tools or playing sports.

7. Notice which students are usually responded to first in discussions and why. Modify any patterns of gender bias.

8. Ask equally challenging questions of female and male students.

9. Use cooperative and competitive learning techniques.

10. Vary instructional strategies.

11. Invite guest speakers into the classroom whose skills break stereotypic gender boundaries.

12. Encourage students to consider nontraditional curricular and career choices.

SUGGESTIONS FOR FURTHER INFORMATION ABOUT GENDER EQUITY

Commonwealth of Australia. (2006). *Success for boys.* Available at http://www.successforboys.edu.au/boys

> This Australian Web site is part of that government's Success for Boys initiative. The resources at this site are divided into five sections, each of which can be downloaded. They contain research-based strategies for teachers to implement in their classrooms and schools. Topics address boys and literacy, mentoring for success, and effective practices for working with indigenous groups.

Helping middle school students make the transition into high school. Available at www.kidsource.com/education/middlehigh.html

> This ERIC Digest provides an overview of select research on transitioning to high school. It addresses the topics of informing students and parents about high school programs, providing students with social support for successful transitions, nurturing collaboration between middle and high school educators, and involving parents in the middle to high school transition process.

Mead, S. (2006). *The evidence suggests otherwise: The truth about boys and girls.* Washington, DC: Education Sector.

> In this report (which is also available for free at www.educationsector.org/usr_doc/ESO_BoysAndGirls.pdf), Sara Mead of the Education Sector critiques the current public debate about boys' achievement, and observes that girls have recently closed many former achievement gaps. She analyzes the trends and implications of the long-term National Assessment of Educational Progress (NAEP), as well as topics of male and female student attainment, aspirations, and educational outcomes. She outlines current theories of the causes of gender differences and offers policy and leadership perspectives.

Neu, T. W., & Weinfeld, R. (2007). *Helping boys succeed in school: A practical guide for parents and teachers.* Waco, TX: Prufrock Press.

> This book combines field-tested strategies and case studies to help parents and teachers improve the achievement of male students. Neu and Weinfeld address several topics, which include:
> - Strategies for channeling boys' interests
> - How to keep boys actively engaged in classroom activities
> - Ways to increase male students' participation in language arts
> - Tips to assist boys in addressing the unique social and emotional problems they encounter in school

The authors include discussions on topics such as mentoring, bullying, and engaging boys with reading and writing.

4

Teaching Diverse Students

Addressing Language, Class, Culture, and Ability Differences in the Classroom

THE DIVERSITY OF THE U.S. EDUCATIONAL SYSTEM

The United States educational system is vast and diverse. During the 2007–2008 school year, the U.S. Department of Education (National Center for Educational Statistics, 2007) reported that 49.6 million K–12 students attended our nation's public schools. Of these, 34.5 million were in Grades preK–8, and another 15 million were in Grades 9 to 12. The 49 million students were housed in approximately 97,000 schools located in 15,000 districts and taught by 3.2 million teachers. In addition, 1.1 million students were homeschooled in the 2007–2008 school year, and 6.1 million students were enrolled in 28,000 private elementary and secondary schools. Finally, 887,000 students were enrolled in charter schools.

In 2007, America's 97,000 public schools were configured in numerous ways (U.S. Department of Education, 2007). The formats consisted primarily of regular, alternative, charter, magnet, Title I, special education, and vocational schools, with considerable variation in size. Whether a school is large or small, alternative or regular, elementary or secondary, rural or urban, a commonly shared purpose, articulated in the No Child Left Behind Act (NCLB) (U.S. Department of Education, 2008), is to ensure that all students gain the knowledge, skills, and information to contribute successfully to their communities throughout their lives. This national goal, while easy to state, is challenging to achieve. Regular classroom teachers endeavor to accommodate a growing student population with multiple languages, unique backgrounds and family lives, and varying academic abilities and interests. Just exactly how diverse is our country's K–12 population?

THE DIVERSITY OF K–12 STUDENTS IN THE UNITED STATES

The U.S. Department of Education (National Center for Educational Statistics, 2008), U.S. Census Bureau (2001), National Clearinghouse for English Language Acquisition (2002), and National Center for Children in Poverty (2001) track four significant categories of student diversity that we address in this chapter: (a) racial, (b) academic, (c) socioeconomic, and (d) linguistic diversity. Though these terms may appear self-evident, there is often considerable confusion about what such concepts actually mean. As a result, federal definitions are provided for each of the four concepts below—as well as for other data of interest to administrators and teachers.

DEFINING RACIAL DIVERSITY

Since 1977, the federal government has used five categories to collect racial data (U. S. Department of Education, 1998). These categories consist of American Indian or Alaskan Native, Asian or Pacific Islander, black, white, and Hispanic. Since the late 1970s, however, the nation's population has grown more diverse, immigration has reached historic levels, and interracial marriages have increased. New terms such as biracial, multiracial, mixed heritage, and others have been suggested as additional racial categories. In the 2005 school year (the last for which data are available), 42 percent of public school students in the United States were minority: 15.6 percent black, 19.7 percent Hispanic, 3.7 percent Asian, .2 percent Pacific Islander, .7 percent Native American or Alaska Native, and 2.5 percent of more than one race.

DEFINING THE CONCEPT OF STUDENTS WITH DISABILITIES

Students with disabilities are those who have individualized education plans (IEPs) as required by the federal Individuals With Disabilities Education Act (IDEA) Amendments (1997), originally the Education for All Handicapped Children Act (1975). IDEA has specified multiple classifications of disability. They include mental retardation or developmental delays; learning problems; behavior or emotional disorders; communication disorders; hearing, speech, or language impairments; visual, physical and other health impairments; severe and multiple disabilities; autism; and traumatic brain injury (U.S. Department of Education, Office of Special Education and Rehabilitative Services, 2007).

The number of students with disabilities receiving special-education services has grown steadily since a national count began in 1976. From 1990 to 2000, the number of students with special needs jumped 30 percent, a rate that was faster than both school enrollment and population growth (U.S. Department of Education, Office of Special Education and Rehabilitative Services, 2000). This increase to over 670,000 as of 2007 (National Center for Education Statistics, 2007) has been attributed to better diagnosis and classification. Slightly under half, or 43 percent, of the students with disabilities were classified as having specific learning disabilities. The three other most prevalent forms of disability included speech and language impairments (22 percent), mental retardation (9 percent), and emotional disturbances (7 percent).

The 1998–1999 school year was the first time that the states were required to report the race and ethnicity of students served under IDEA. As a result, it was determined that white and Asian students were underrepresented in the special-education population while blacks and American Indian students were overrepresented. Hispanic students were represented at a rate comparable to the population.

DEFINING STUDENTS IN POVERTY

The National Center for Children in Poverty (2007) reported that children are more likely to live in poverty than any other age group in America and that their numbers have increased since 1979. In 2007, the federal poverty line for a family of four was $20,650 of annual income, and at that time, approximately 17 percent of American school-aged children, or 28.6 million, lived in or near poverty. Research shows that, on average, families need an income of about twice that level to cover basic expenses. Using this standard, 39 percent of children in the United States live in low-income families (National Center for Children in Poverty, 2007).

The younger the child, the greater the risk of poverty, evidenced with 42 percent of children under age 6 living in low-income families, whereas 33 percent of adolescents live in such families. Half the states have early childhood poverty rates of more than 20 percent. Research tells us that experiencing poverty in early childhood, along with persistent poverty, is the most harmful to children (Testimony on the Economic and Societal Costs of Poverty, House Ways and Means Committee, January, 2007). Seven percent of children fared even worse by living in extreme poverty, the term used for a family of three in 1999 that earned $6,145 or less annually. Research has shown that extreme poverty during the first five years of life has greater negative effects for future life opportunities than extreme poverty later in childhood.

The category of impoverished children also encompasses those who are homeless. The Stewart B. McKinney Homeless Assistance Act of 1988 (Legal Information Institute, Cornell University, n. d.) federally defined the homeless as individuals who lack fixed, regular, or adequate residences. A fixed residence is permanent and unchanging. A regular residence is used consistently, and an adequate one meets the psychological and physical needs of a home. Examples of homeless students include those in emergency, runaway, or transitional shelters; those living in deserted buildings or on the streets; those staying temporarily in camping grounds or trailer parks; those waiting for permanent placement by state agencies; or those abandoned by their families. While only estimates are available of the number of homeless adults and children, the U.S. Department of Education reported that approximately 700,000 K–12 students were homeless during 1998 (National Center for Homeless Education, n.d.). Though assumed to be an urban problem, approximately one third of the homeless are in rural areas (Vissing, 1996). As might be expected, due, in part, to the irregularity of their attendance, many homeless students encounter significant educational challenges.

DEFINING LIMITED ENGLISH PROFICIENT STUDENTS

Limited English proficient (LEP) students, also referred to as language minority students or English language learners (ELL), are those living in households where a language other than English is the primary language. Language minority students are the fastest growing population in U.S. schools, and they represent a broad spectrum of language proficiency (Ovando & Collier, 1998; Ovando, Collier & Combs, 2003). Such students range from indigenous minorities whose ancestors have lived in North America for tens of thousands of years to recent immigrants from countries around the world. Twenty percent of all U.S. students speak a first language other than English (National Center for Education Statistics, 2007).

Title IX of the No Child Left Behind Act of 2001 legally defines Limited English proficient (LEP) students. According to Title IX, General Provisions, Part A Definitions, Section 9101(25), an LEP student is a child

> whose difficulties in speaking, reading, writing, or understanding the English language may be sufficient to deny the individual the ability to meet the state's proficient level of achievement on state assessments; the ability to successfully achieve in classrooms where the language of instruction is English; or the opportunity to participate fully in society.

As such, they are entitled to identification and placement services. Services may include bilingual or English as a Second Language (ESL) programs. To distinguish between these two services: Bilingual programs provide some native-language content instruction while students also learn English during part of the school day. In ESL programs, students receive content instruction in English and are pulled out of the classroom for part of the day to learn English skills with other LEP students. In the 2003–04 school year, English language learner (ELL) services were provided to 3.8 million students (11 percent of all students) (U.S. Department of Education, National Center for Education Statistics, 2006). The U.S. Department of Education (2001b) reported that ESL programs were more common than bilingual programs and that 13 percent of schools enrolling LEP students have neither program. It should be noted that while the term LEP is used extensively in literature and demographic data, some prefer the use of English Language Teaching (ELT), since it avoids connoting deficiency until full English proficiency is attained (Ovando & Collier, 1998).

During the decade from 1990 to 2000, the National Clearinghouse for English Language Acquisition (2002) reported that the numbers of LEP students have more than doubled from 2 million in 1990 to over 4 million in 2000.

As of 2000, about three fourths of the students spoke Spanish; the nine other largest groups, in descending order, were Vietnamese, Hmong, Cantonese, Cambodian, Korean, Laotian, Navajo, Tagalog, and Russian. Demographic projections indicate that language diversity among K–12 students will continue to increase. A summary of data is displayed in Table 4.1.

IMPLICATIONS OF STUDENT DIVERSITY FOR THE CLASSROOM

All K–12 students are entitled to access, equity, and quality academic experiences. Equitable education can be best accomplished through inclusive classrooms that respond to student differences. Such classrooms underscore a fundamental truth about any group of students or people, as Howard Gardner's (2003) work, cited previously, has also emphasized: that not everyone functions at an equivalent level in all subjects or areas of cognitive challenge. Inclusive classrooms address student differences while seeking to develop skills and abilities that prevent social stratification, an important educational and societal goal (Hallahan & Kauffman, 1994; Oakes, 1985; Page, 1991; Slavin, 1987; Wheelock, 1992).

Fortunately, there is a body of literature that can be relied on for the effective instruction of a wide array of student needs. The teaching practices described in this chapter fall under the broad umbrella of inclusive instruction. In this chapter, we summarize some of what has been learned about teaching approaches that result in positive achievement gains for diverse students. And we give examples of instructional techniques that target specific groups of students, such as LEP or special needs. In practice, however, the majority of strategies can be used in most classrooms.

Table 4.1   K–12 Student Diversity in the United States

Category	Approximate K–12 Student Numbers Based on 47,000,000	Approximate Percentage of K–12 Student Population
Racial Diversity		
Among Students		
American Indian		
and Alaska Natives	500,000	1%
Asian and Pacific Islanders	2,000,000	4%
Hispanics	7,000,000	16%
Blacks	8,000,000	17%
Whites	29,000,000	62%
Students With Disabilities:		
All K–12 students	6,000,000	12%
Students in Poverty:		
All K–12 students	8,000,000	17%
Homeless K–12 students	700,000	1%
Limited English		
Proficient Students		
All K–12 students	4,000,000	8%

TEACHING STUDENTS WITH SPECIAL NEEDS IN MAINSTREAM CLASSROOMS

Teacher attitudes and attributes have proven to be an important predictor for the achievement of students with special needs (Baum, Renzulli, & Hebert, 1995; Coates, 1989; Idol, Nevin, & Paolucci-Whitcomb, 1994; Olson, Chalmers, & Hoover, 1997). Teachers who are skilled at effectively teaching a range of students in the same classroom have been found to be tolerant, reflective, and flexible. They accept responsibility for the academic success of all students and demonstrate high academic expectations, a relentless pursuit of excellence in teaching and are warm and accepting in their interactions with students (Haberman, 1995).

In addition to positive personal characteristics, many inclusive teachers employ powerful instructional techniques. One such strategy is tiered instruction, also known as "leveling" (Collicott, 1991) or "multilevel instruction" (Johnson, 1999). Likewise, tutoring can be remarkably effective in raising achievement among students with learning disabilities and others behind in grade level skills (Educational Research Service, 2004; Erlbaum, Moody, Vaughn, Schumm, & Hughes, 1999; Gersten, Baker, Marks, & Smith, 1999; U.S. Department of Education, 1997a). All of us, at times, benefit from reflecting on whether we understand what is being taught. Monitoring learning can prevent students from slipping further behind in their studying (Nelson-Le Gall, 1985; Schumm, Vaughn, & Sobol, 1997).

Effective, inclusive teachers also target reading as an essential skill and work to ensure strong literacy achievement of all students. For example, one research study showed that a daily reading course included in an urban multiethnic high school curriculum yielded reading achievement gains four times those of those students not taking the course (Allington, 2001).

Inclusive teachers also consider ways to meet the needs of gifted students in the classroom. Since there are no federal guidelines for defining gifted students, the identification of such students is locally determined by schools, districts and, in some cases, at the state level. Gifted children can be found in all racial, language, and socioeconomic groups, and they tend to share some or all of the following characteristics: they learn quickly, are highly motivated, have excellent memories, perceive relationships, and may demonstrate advanced skills or knowledge of a discipline (Frasier & Passow, 1994; Subotnik & LeBlanc, 2001). Gifted students benefit from instruction that accommodates their intense curiosity. Strategies later in this chapter offer ways to nurture their talents within the regular classroom.

INTEGRATING LIMITED ENGLISH PROFICIENT STUDENTS INTO MAINSTREAM CLASSROOMS

Not enough teachers have been trained to work with language minority students. As a result, educators are left to improvise and intentionally seek out professional development. Fortunately, recent research has identified effective approaches that monolingual, mainstream teachers can use in their classrooms. To begin, teachers can intentionally modulate their use of English to improve the comprehension of those who are learning our language (Brice & Roseberry-McKibbin, 1999; Gersten et al., 1999). Second, teachers can monitor the vocabulary they teach to English-learning students and intentionally emphasize academic terms most needed in schools. As was explained in Chapter 1, vocabulary plays a fundamental role in any student's knowledge base and academic success (Marzano, 2004, 2005). Teachers can use Strategies #16, 17, and 18 from Chapter 1 to teach key concepts. This will develop the background knowledge of their ELL and all students simultaneously.

A longitudinal study that spanned 14 years—from 1982 to 1996—and surveyed the records of 700,000 language minority students revealed instructional methods that promoted strong achievement gains (Thomas & Collier, 1997). Not surprisingly, these included collaborative, interactive, interdisciplinary, and discovery approaches to learning. Such examples are described later in this chapter and are also evident in Chapter 2 on Active Learning.

Another group of ELL students deserving special attention are those who may be preliterate. Such circumstances often arise when students did not have the opportunity to attend school in their former countries or to learn how to read and write in their native languages. Strategies for meeting these students' needs are also addressed in this chapter.

TEACHING RACIALLY DIVERSE STUDENTS

Over the last several years, schools and teachers have successfully grappled with many aspects of multicultural education. This is evident in classroom efforts to prepare students to live in an ethnically diverse society by making the curriculum responsive to the experiences, traditions, and historical and contemporary contributions of many groups represented in our nation's population. Additionally, many educators and researchers claim that multicultural education also leads to enhanced academic achievement (Gay, 2001; Revilla & Sweeney, 1997; Webb, 1990). In this chapter, multicultural perspectives are infused into discussions of mathematics and literature studies. Through such efforts, not only do minority students benefit but so also do majority students whose appreciation for the tapestry of American life is broadened and deepened.

There is tremendous language diversity across the United States. Both the numbers of language minority students and nonstandard English speakers are increasing. Many students speak black English, Appalachian English, Indian English, and Hawaiian Creole, to name a few dialects. Nonstandard English usage is also prevalent among diverse social classes (Joos, 1972; Payne, 1995). Schools and teachers can successfully teach formal English while affirming the importance of students' home dialects and encouraging them to communicate in both languages, as appropriate. Strategies addressing this issue will be found later in the chapter.

TEACHING STUDENTS IN POVERTY

While being poor does not necessarily equate with underachievement, students in poverty do bring special needs to schools. Fortunately, research on Title I schools (Diamond & Moore, 1993; Revilla & Sweeney, 1997) and Haberman's (1995, 2004) three decades of studies on "star teachers" of children of poverty reveal teacher characteristics and instructional strategies that boost the performance of disadvantaged children.

Some children in poverty move frequently. While changing schools can occasionally yield positive effects, such as taking advantage of a fresh start socially or accessing new academic programs, frequent mobility usually results in negative consequences. Students who are highly transient are at greater risk for underachievement, misbehavior, and youth violence (Educational Research Service, 2001). Mobility also adversely affects schools by slowing the pace of instruction, lowering teacher morale, and adding to administrative loads. While it is unlikely that student mobility will suddenly decrease, schools and teachers can take steps to mitigate some of its harmful effects (Arroyo, Rhoad, & Drew, 1999; Educational Research Service, 2001).

REFLECTING ON TEACHING IN DIVERSE CLASSROOMS

Perhaps more than any other phenomenon in education, the diversity of K–12 students serves as the greatest catalyst for professional growth (Johnson, 2006). While U.S. teachers are predominantly white, female, and middle-class, particularly in elementary schools, our students represent an array of linguistic, racial, academic, and socioeconomic groups. The diversity in the classroom encourages us to confront our beliefs about those we teach. We can ponder questions such as: What are my assumptions about diverse groups? Where did I acquire such notions? How do these beliefs influence my attitudes toward my students and instruction? What do I need to unlearn and learn? The rest of this chapter puts tools into teachers' hands to work more successfully with all students in the classroom.

#66: TIERED INSTRUCTION

Using Tiered Instruction: Adjusting Lessons for Different Ability Levels

Tiered instruction is an instructional technique that teaches one skill or concept at varying levels of challenge or various learning profiles. It provides diverse ways of learning for students in mixed-ability classrooms so that all students are challenged, use higher level thinking skills, and make significant achievement gains (Richards, 2005). Tiered instruction is sometimes referred to as leveled instruction, scaffolded instruction, or layered instruction. There are several models of tiered instruction but no consensus as to which model or formula is definitive.

Nonetheless, a well-designed tiered lesson ensures that students with different learning needs have the opportunity to work with the same concepts or skills at levels appropriate to their abilities. The lesson's tiers vary the complexity of work that students are to do, rather than the quantity of work they are expected to complete. Consider two students in a math class. Student A struggles with basic concepts and mathematical reasoning and often needs help understanding the principles of a lesson. Student B has advanced beyond the same concepts, in fact beyond grade level, yet still needs to be challenged in mathematics. Clearly, a single approach will not suffice since they are at different levels. Student A will not receive the help he needs to understand the basic ideas being presented. Student B is unlikely to be sufficiently challenged. The basic principles or standards targeted in a lesson may be the same, but students A and B may approach them from different directions or at different levels of difficulty. In a tiered lesson, both students A and B should have the opportunity to learn the skills or principles of the lesson, both should be supported in their learning, and both should be appropriately challenged.

There is no designated number of tiers in a tiered lesson: three tiers or three levels is common, however, there may be only two or, on occasion, four or more. Models of instruction with three tiers usually have one tier for students below standard or grade level, one at standard or grade level, and the third above standard or grade level. Typically the students in any classroom may not fall into three categories, so teachers will need to adjust the number of tiers in planning a lesson.

Listed below are four models of tiered instruction. Each can be easily adapted to suit a teacher's need.

1. The leveled model

    The most traditional model, which divides a class into three groups or tiers:
    - Tier 1—Multiple approaches to basic facts, skills, vocabulary, techniques, etc.
    - Tier 2—Activities or projects applying knowledge and skills from Tier 1
    - Tier 3—Critical analysis and/or real-world applications of knowledge and skills

2. The to-with-by model

Scaffolds learning in three tiers:
- Direct instruction, where students are presented a new skill or concept (to)
- Guided instruction, where students practice with teacher support (with)
- Individualized learning, where students extend learning independently (by)

3. The Bloom's model

Based on Benjamin Bloom's Taxonomy of Higher-Order Thinking Skills:
- Tier 2—Begin where most students are with comprehension and analysis activities
- Tier 1—Tier down for students struggling with basic skills or concepts
- Tier 3—Tier up for students capable of higher-level thinking (e.g., synthesis, evaluation)

4. The contract or layered model

Based on the idea that only students demonstrating mastery should move to higher tiers:
- Tier 1—All students participate in basic instructional activities
- Tier 2—Students who master Tier 1 extend their learning
- Tier 3—Students who master Tier 2 further extend their learning

Response to Intervention (RTI) (U.S. Department of Education, 2007), articulated in the recent reauthorization of IDEA, also suggests a three-tier model of instruction. The RTI approach to tiered instruction is open-ended and can include any of the models listed above. The concept can also serve as a framework for thinking about RTI. Vaughn and Wanzek (2007) explain:

> The 3-tier framework can be adjusted for any research-based program and any grouping practice. For example, students can be provided interventions in a range of group sizes including whole class, small group, pairs, and one-on-one. Students can be grouped within class, within grade or across grade as appropriate. Any grouping practices associated with the efficacy of a research-based program are appropriate. Interventions delivered within the 3-tier framework may also vary in the amount of time they are delivered per day based on students' needs and students' responses to intervention.

Regardless of the model, tiered instruction enables academically diverse students to work on similar curriculum at levels appropriate to their abilities (see Figure 4.1). Any lesson can accommodate varying degrees of complexity and depth.

Because of limited time in busy teachers' schedules, tiering can be done by a teacher, a group of teachers at a grade level or in a subject, or teachers in special workshops outside the school. It may not be possible to reformat all lessons. When tiering is desired, the following can guide lesson development. This information is adapted from the work of Collicott (1991, pp. 191–218).

- Consider the specific knowledge or skills to be taught. These may be based on state standards or district curriculum guidelines.
- Determine how to informally preassess students' knowledge and skills.
- Identify an instructional strategy for presenting the content of the lesson. Based on teaching experience, textbook recommendations, or input from colleagues, use a strategy that will effectively incorporate the specific components of the knowledge or skill being targeted.
- Visualize a range of knowledge or ability, from students with minimal understanding of the content to advanced understanding. How broad or deep is their prior knowledge? How complex are their skills? Consider how your identified strategy will meet the needs of students along this continuum.
- Determine how you will modify your designated activity for various students in your class. Two versions may be enough, but depending on the range of students, it may take three or even more versions. The modifications may involve different materials, groupings, vocabulary, rates of presentation, or entry points to the lesson.
- Align each student or group of students in the class with a corresponding modification in the lesson. Make sure that each student's needs are addressed and that each student is appropriately challenged.
- Identify a meaningful and appropriate assessment activity. Since students learn at different levels, they should have the opportunity to demonstrate their learning at different levels.

Figure 4.1 Tiering Curriculum

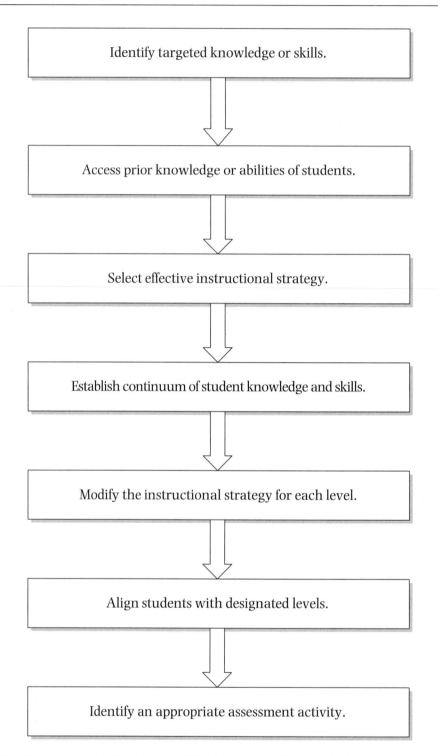

SOURCE: Adapted from J. Collicott (1991).

#67: TIERED SPELLING

The following tiered spelling strategy teaches one lesson while encouraging varied student experiences and responses. As such, it is appropriate for use with gifted or challenged students, the learning disabled, or ELLs. Students develop individualized spelling lists from three sources: (a) teacher-generated words, (b) student-identified words from academic content, and (c) student-identified words from everyday life or their career interests. They also problem-solve their own strategies for accurate spelling. This strategy is adapted from the work of Johnson (1999, p. 76).

1. Generate and distribute a spelling list of approximately 10 to 20 words.

2. Ask students to add to your list by identifying five or more spelling words they want to learn from diverse subject areas. Teachers may assist some students in compiling such lists.

3. Ask students to add five or more words from their everyday lives or from their career interests. Each student should provide the teacher with an individualized list of five discipline-based words and five career or everyday spelling words.

4. Once the spelling lists are compiled, organize students into heterogeneous groups of approximately three or four. Include one strong speller, one weak speller, and one or two average spellers in each group.

5. While in their groups, ask students to brainstorm effective approaches to studying their spelling words. Encourage each student to contribute at least one strategy, and suggest that the groups be creative. They can use color, shape, size, and sound when working with their words; or create mnemonic devices, flash cards, or games. After their discussions, ask the groups to select a person to compile a list of each member's suggested strategies.

6. Ask that the small groups explain or demonstrate one or more of their techniques to the class. Once the groups have shared, compile a comprehensive list of suggested spelling-word strategies, and later distribute the list to all students.

7. When students have received the combined list of suggestions for studying spelling words, the teacher should select a few to discuss, demonstrate, and practice with the entire class.

8. Next, ask students to select strategies to use when studying their words. Such techniques may be individualized approaches or include teacher or peer assistance.

9. Plan to set aside some class time for students to study their spelling words. Some may work independently, with partners, or in small groups. Markers, note cards, and other resources should be available as needed.

10. During the study session, move from student to student or group to group to support and clarify processes and to assist students in assessing their spelling improvement. Students will likely be engaged in a variety of activities during such sessions. For example, a pair may have made spelling games and be receiving feedback on their efforts. Other pairs may ask each other to orally spell selected words. Some may write paragraphs using specific words.

11. After the study sessions, ask the class to discuss the most effective studying strategies, perhaps generating a top five or ten list.

12. Assess students' spelling skills individually through written or oral means.

#68: DO THEY GET IT? ASSESSING STUDENT UNDERSTANDING IN INCLUSIVE CLASSROOMS

As teachers know all too well, once a lesson begins, some students exhibit confusion or disengagement. Research shows that the lower the students' achievement, the more reluctant they are to reveal their lack of understanding (Nelson-Le Gall, 1985). Teachers should be vigilant about checking in with students to see if they understand assignments, lectures, or homework. Several monitoring techniques are suggested in this strategy, which are appropriate for highly diverse student groups.

Ask Content and Process Questions

Asking both content and process questions can strengthen questioning during class time. Content questions ask, "What is the answer?" while process questions ask, "How did you arrive at that answer?"

Circulate Around the Room

Research shows that effective teachers move around the classroom to monitor students and their work. Such informal observations give teachers opportunities to gauge student understanding and intervene quickly as needed.

Ensure Understanding at the Beginning of an Assignment

Make sure students understand concepts and directions at the beginning of a lesson to ward off confusion and mistakes. You might ask students to rephrase your directions, summarize the steps of a task, or ask clarifying questions.

Check Student Understanding at Frequent Intervals

Ask students to summarize key points of a task at frequent intervals. This lets the teacher observe whether students are on track or need redirection.

Encourage Students to Ask Questions

Make asking questions a classroom norm. Encourage students, especially those who struggle, to ask clarifying questions. When introducing or practicing a complex concept, remind students that learning is challenging and that asking questions or requesting assistance can improve learning.

Use Feedback Forms

Distribute prepared feedback forms at the beginning of a lesson. They can include phrases such as, "It was easy for me to . . . ," "What 1 learned was . . . ," "What I don't understand is . . . ," "I am confused about . . . ," "I would like to review. . . ." Students can use these forms during a lesson to record their reactions and hand them in at the end of a lesson.

Give Practice Tests

Before an actual test, give students a practice test to see what they have learned. The tests should be short and brief. They can be open- or closed-book and administered to students individually, in pairs, or in small groups. Students can use practice tests to review what they have learned and to identify what needs to be studied further. Feedback should be immediate.

SOURCE: "Are They Getting it? How to Monitor Student Understanding in Inclusive Classrooms" by J. S. Schumm, S. Vaughn, & M. C. Sobol (1997, January). *Intervention in School and Clinic, 32*(3), 168–171. Copyright by PRO-ED, Inc. Adapted with permission.

#69: TEACHING ELEMENTARY READERS

Primary-grade teachers have the enormous responsibility of teaching children to read. While some students will learn to read almost effortlessly, others require explicit and focused instruction. Research has identified approaches to preventing reading problems among young students. Some of that information is synthesized in the following checklist of 11 suggestions that teachers of Grades 1–3 can use to ensure the literacy achievement of all students. Check all the listed items that reflect your current efforts, and put a star by any approaches that you would like to add.

To teach reading in my classroom, I consistently:

1. Teach and model letter and sound skills and spelling-sound correspondences (Pressley et al., 2001; Snow et al., 1998)

2. Teach high frequency or sight recognition words (Snow et al., 1998)

3. Encourage children to write often (Snow et al., 1998)

4. Support students' initial use of invented spelling and develop correct spelling through focused instruction and practice (Snow et al., 1998)

5. Provide a rich literacy environment with two types of instructional materials: (a) those that students can easily read to themselves and (b) those that students can learn to read with assistance (Snow et al., 1998)

6. Encourage those students who are beginning to read independently to sound out and confirm unfamiliar words rather than relying on context clues alone (Snow et al., 1998)

7. Teach two or more reading skills during each hour of reading instruction, and design lessons so students spend much more time reading and writing than preparing or following up (Pressley et al., 2001)

8. Explicitly teach comprehension strategies, such as summarizing the main idea, predicting events and outcomes, creating mental images, drawing inferences, and monitoring for coherence and misunderstandings (Pressley et al., 2001; Snow et al., 1998)

9. Teach students to plan, draft, and revise as part of the writing process (Pressley et al., 2001)

10. Promote reading and writing outside school through daily, at-home assignments and expectations, summer activities, and inclusion of parents and others, such as public librarians (Snow et al., 1998)

#70: HELPING STRUGGLING INTERMEDIATE READERS

Some children make adequate progress during the primary grades with reading but later encounter difficulties. It is professionally responsible to assume that many students will require ongoing support with literacy achievement. Strategies derived from the research of Allington (2001) and the U.S. Department of Education's National Institute for Literacy (2000) target struggling intermediate-level readers for assistance. Several classroom approaches are listed below.

1. Plan to provide struggling readers with four types of support: (a) access to books at appropriate reading and interest levels, (b) long-term support from a reading specialist or resource or development center, (c) extra support for reading in the content areas (see Activity # 71), and (d) school-family reading coordination.

2. Expand instructional time for reading. Add a second daily reading lesson taught by the classroom or specialist teacher or offer before- or after-school programs.

3. Assess students' reading ability frequently. Particularly target their comprehension and their fluency, and, when problems are noted, plan instruction or assistance accordingly.

4. Focus on enhancing vocabulary. Some students benefit when their teachers take dictation of their statements. The students read what they have said and memorize spelling and punctuation accordingly. To help students develop extensive sight vocabularies, some teachers make lists of words from age-appropriate selections they read aloud. Each student has a box of index cards and keeps adding selected words to study. Later, they use these words in narrative and expository writing.

5. Model reading and comprehension strategies for students, and post such techniques on bulletin boards or walls.

6. Vary student opportunities for reading. Ask them to read in pairs and small groups. Also ask students to read out loud by first skimming a text for answers and then reading aloud the words or phrases that provide the answers to questions posed in class.

7. Vary the types of materials students are asked to read, such as stories, reports, letters, newspapers, and Web site information.

#71: TEACHING READING IN THE CONTENT AREAS

Providing support for students in content area classes is an important component of a systemic approach to strong literacy achievement. Content area teachers do not have to forgo their subject matter to focus on reading. Instead, they can explicitly integrate reading supports into everyday instruction. When they do, students have greater opportunities to work with grade-level materials and to avoid confusion and frustration when reading text materials. Several suggestions for content area teachers follow.

1. Think about your instruction of new content as having three phases. The first activates students' background knowledge, the second constructs new knowledge, and the third asks students to apply and use the new knowledge.

2. Model and discuss your own reading processes to make them explicit for students. Perhaps you might explain that, after reading a page or two, you stop to summarize key ideas in your own words.

3. Give students a clear purpose or goal for reading.

4. Ask what students may already know about the topic and apply that knowledge to the text to be read.

5. Define key terms, interpret important phrases, and ask students to look for them when they read.

6. With students working individually at first, ask them to predict what they think the five or ten most important words will be in a reading selection. Next, put students in pairs to cooperatively develop their top five or ten words. Ask all students to read the material, to note the important concepts, and, in pairs, to revise their original lists.

7. Explain text features, such as headings, graphs, and pictures, that can help students predict the content of the text. Ask them to make and test predictions,

8. Ask students to keep a journal in which they write out definitions and explore important concepts.

9. Set aside time for reflection on what was read. Ask students to summarize main ideas in sections of text or to make charts, outlines, or webs of the content they covered.

10. Encourage recreational reading of high-interest materials, such as sports statistics for math or science-fiction books for science.

#72: HELPING STRUGGLING ADOLESCENT READERS

Weak reading ability, rather than illiteracy, is a common concern of many secondary-level teachers. According to the 2004 National Assessment of Educational Progress (NAEP) (U.S. Department of Education, National Center for Educational Statistics, n.d.), about one fourth of 8th graders and one fifth of 12th graders read below the basic level. This means that they do not understand the main ideas of a text, make inferences, or relate what they have read to their personal lives. Some secondary schools are developing approaches to improving the reading achievement of their students through a reading apprentice approach (Association for Supervision and Curriculum Development, 2000; Educational Research Service, 2001). Some apprentice activities are described below.

Reading Apprenticeships

Teachers serve as "master readers" and work with students who are "apprentice readers" to analyze the reading process and teach how to read nonliterary texts.

1. Students are taught metacognitive skills to identify what they do and don't understand when confronted with a variety of texts.

2. Together, students and teachers sometimes work their way through a reading selection and use reciprocal-teaching techniques. These include predicting, clarifying, questioning, and summarizing. To clarify what they have read, for example, students might reread portions of the text or discuss them in small groups, then read further in the text to see if the meaning becomes clear, or connect what they are reading with their lives.

3. The teacher asks students to examine ten or more unidentified text excerpts. These might include selections taken from a job application, a tax form, a magazine quiz, academic texts, directions for assembling a computer, or samples of commercial writing. Students are asked to categorize each selection, identify its use, and rate their understanding of each item. They then must decide which reading skills to use to improve their understanding of the difficult texts.

4. Twice weekly, students engage in sustained silent reading with self-selected materials. Some of this reading will be in school, and some will be outside school hours—in a reading club after school or at home. They must maintain weekly reading logs, read 200 pages a month, and do monthly culminating projects in which they reflect on themselves as readers.

#73: USING TUTORS TO INCREASE READING ACHIEVEMENT

Well-designed tutoring programs that use volunteers and nonprofessionals as tutors can significantly raise students' reading achievement (Educational Research Service, 2008; U.S. Department of Education, 1997a). Research consistently shows that several forms of tutoring, whether peer, cross-age, or adult tutoring, can improve the reading achievement of the disadvantaged, students with mild disabilities, and ELLs. Teachers or schools wanting to implement effective tutoring options for their remedial readers can choose from among the models of effective programs listed below.

Connect Tutoring Content With Classroom Reading Instruction

Students perform better when tutors align their efforts with good classroom-reading practices. The tutoring should be in line with classroom instruction. Structured sessions that contain opportunities for rereading classroom materials, analyzing words, and allowing writing opportunities are beneficial.

Provide Tutors With Ongoing Training

Tutors who receive training and feedback throughout their participation attain better results with students than those who do not receive such coaching. Important topics to cover with tutors include tips for establishing positive interpersonal relationships with students, strategies for reinforcing correct responses and correcting mistakes, ways to structure the tutoring sessions, and how to model reading and writing processes. Reading specialists might provide such training and oversight.

Offer Frequent Tutoring Sessions

Successful tutoring programs run from 10 to 30 minutes and pair the same tutor and tutee three times weekly. This frequency of sessions generates greater achievement than tutoring that is scheduled twice weekly or less.

Use a Variety of Tutors

Studies have shown that a wide variety of people can effectively serve as tutors. Peer or cross-age tutors can effectively improve reading skills of their tutees. Even at-risk middle school LEP students have successfully tutored low-achieving elementary students and improved their own skills in the process.

College students, paraprofessionals, retirees, volunteers, and parents can all work effectively as tutors with support and oversight.

Design Interventions for Students With Disabilities

Trained volunteers with careful supervision from reading or resource teachers can successfully work with students with severe reading difficulties. In such cases, a certified reading specialist can assess children's reading skills and needs, develop lesson plans, observe tutors, and provide them with feedback. Important strategies for improving reading and learning among struggling readers include instilling an appreciation of written material, printed language, and the writing system; teaching the alphabet; developing students' phonological skills and phonemic awareness; teaching phonics, spelling, and vocabulary skills; and fluency and reflective reading.

Provide Ongoing Assessment of Tutored Students

Frequently assess students' reading skills so that tutoring can be tailored to meet their individual needs.

#74: AN EXTRA NET: USING WEB SITES TO SUPPORT THE NEEDS OF DIVERSE LEARNERS

There are a growing number of educationally sound sites available on the Internet. The sites listed below are maintained by credible organizations and offer content that matches common curricular goals. Their content provides both practice and enrichment for a variety of students. Make certain, however, before students access the Internet at school, that your building has an Acceptable Use Policy in place and that parents or caregivers have given written permission for their children to use the Internet.

Mathematics

- Math assistance in all areas: http://www.math.com/students/practice .html. Offers help in basic math, everyday math, algebra, geometry, fractions, etc.
- Help with algebra: http://www.purplemath.com. Free online tutoring, lessons, quizzes, and more.
- All kinds of math assistance: http://www.geocities.com/ivonebl/mathhelp .html. Everything from help for girls to calculus.

Language Arts

- Language arts help and more: http://www.infoplease.com/homework/ hwenglish.html. Provides help in spelling, grammar, literature, authors, poets, poetry, and in other subjects.
- English, language arts homework help: http://www.readingcomprehension connection.com/reading_lesson.php. This interactive site provides online reading comprehension lessons that can be used in the classroom or by students at home.
- Homework help in English: http://www.jiskha.com/english Excellent help on vocabulary, grammar, authors, literary terms, books, novels, etc.
- Vocabulary development for Grades 4–12: http://www.vocabulary.com. Vocabulary is taught through thematic puzzles at three levels of difficulty.
- Writing a research paper: http://www.ipl.org/div/aplus Offers online help for students on research and writing.
- All kinds of writing: http://www.westga.edu/~writing/writing/topreturn 2htm. Gives great support for different writing styles, essays, test preparation, outlines, reports, speech writing, and more.

#75: ENGAGING THE GIFTED

Gifted students often learn more quickly than their peers and want to explore content in greater depth and complexity. Here are 10 techniques to help them jump ahead.

1. With the whole class, brainstorm a list of independent choices students can make when they have successfully completed their work. Post the list in the classroom and encourage students to select one or two activities to pursue when appropriate.

2. Encourage those who have finished work ahead of their peers to pursue additional reading, help other classmates, or go to the library for independent study. Have students who pursue independent reading keep reading logs to hand in for review. Such a log might look like Figure 4.2.

3. Set aside blocks of time in the classroom or library for students to pursue projects and discussions.

4. Secure permission from other teachers for your students to attend their classes as a way to enrich their learning.

5. Accelerate the pace of study in your classroom for gifted students by allowing them to complete assignments at a faster pace.

6. If assignments appear too easy for some students, allow them to demonstrate mastery of the content without extensive practice and drill, and then move on.

7. Extend content by asking students to consider multiple perspectives, current events, or historical components to deepen their knowledge base.

8. Identify an older student or adult mentor to supervise a highly capable student's self-selected project.

9. Occasionally group gifted students together to collaborate on assignments.

10. Identify broad concepts, such as power, conflict, or beauty, and ask students to extend the regular curriculum by thematically considering added dimensions of their studies.

Figure 4.2 Reading Log

Date	Title and Author	Pages: from ___ to ___	Responses: I wonder, predict, question, think, was reminded of, am curious about:

#76: HELPING NEW AND INCOMING STUDENTS

Going to a new school can be a stressful experience for students and their families as well as for classroom teachers. Schools can establish procedures to welcome and engage new students while easing the transition of their relocation, as in the procedures described below and adapted (except for the first #6) from the Educational Research Service (2001, p. 9).

Before a New Student Arrives

1. Have orientation packets to distribute that feature school and teacher profiles, a student handbook, news articles or school newsletters, yearbooks, extracurricular information, and important contact numbers.

2. Establish a newcomers' club to meet once weekly with counselors or others.

3. Administer short basic-skill assessments to identify where a student might best be placed.

4. Maintain packets of core readings or assignments to give to incoming students to orient them to classrooms.

5. Create referral procedures.

6. Plan and host an orientation or open house exclusively for new students and their families. Nearly all students in one study said they appreciated meeting a school staff member before attending classes (Jalongo, 1994).

7. Enlist students' assistance in orienting new classmates to the school.

8. Create a short list of school and classroom procedures.

Ongoing Procedures

1. Explicitly model and explain classroom routines and expectations.

2. Use collaborative learning in the classroom, and foster positive peer interactions.

3. Individualize instruction as needed and provide tutoring or enrichment before or afterschool or during lunch.

4. Address the students' physical and psychosocial needs, and link them with appropriate resources.

5. Articulate student strengths and communicate high expectations.

6. Encourage goal setting and age-appropriate self-determination. Celebrate accomplishments.

7. Contact the parents or caregivers to welcome them to the school and to inform them about classrooms and programs.

8. Offer independent study options for new students to make up missed credits.

9. Maintain portfolios and work samples to document academic growth.

10. Have teachers or students invite newcomers to participate in the school's extracurricular programs.

SOURCE: Adapted from Educational Research Service (2001).

#77: MEETING THE NEEDS OF PRELITERATE ENGLISH LANGUAGE LEARNER STUDENTS

Immigrant or refugee students are appearing in greater numbers in the schools. Some, who have left war-torn countries or suffered catastrophic natural disasters, may not have attended school regularly if at all. As a result, some ELLs may be preliterate and require specialized support. Ten suggestions for improving the achievement of preliterate students are listed below. They are adapted from the work of the Northwest Regional Educational Laboratory (2008).

1. To increase cultural awareness and sensitivity, teachers should learn about the values, traditions, and customs of the students in their classes. This can be accomplished through reading, conducting Internet searches, attending classes, participating in immigrant community events, and having conversations with members of a particular group. Once learned, knowledge of a student's home culture can be integrated into instruction by using culturally familiar examples or topics.

2. Learn about varied immigrant experiences and use such information background knowledge as appropriate to tap in the classroom. One caveat, however, is to consider the fears of undocumented students. Additionally, teachers may want to know their district and state polices regarding information about students' and families' immigration status.

3. Encourage parents or others to read with students in their native languages. Regardless of the language, knowledge of text structure, rhetorical devices, visual-perceptual skills, and cognitive processes transfer from one language to another.

4. Provide one-on-one literacy instruction in the native and English languages. Research shows the best long-term achievement gains occur when students become literate in their primary language first (Ovando & Collier, 1998). Likewise, reading skills can be developed in both languages simultaneously with no negative academic consequences. Teacher aides, student teachers, and volunteers may offer individualized tutoring sessions. Providing personalized attention to older students can help close the achievement gap and prevent them from dropping out of school altogether.

5. Establish a positive and supportive environment that encourages all students to engage in conversational opportunities in the classroom. At the same time, be aware that ELL students may experience a nonverbal or silent period as they develop new language skills and confidence in new settings.

6. Make an effort to learn some vocabulary in the native language of students to better communicate with them. If able, learn key words or phrases to integrate into the instruction of key concepts or skills.

7. Increase students' ability to understand English by selecting familiar topics of conversation, creating a context (see activities in Chapter 1) for what is to be learned, using simple sentence constructions, repeating important phrases, and matching your body language to what you are stating.

8. Enlist the assistance of a school's ESL teacher to provide classes that target cognitive and academic development, oral-language skills, and practice in reading and writing.

9. Encourage your school to offer programs or refer students to programs that extend beyond academics. These might include counseling services that are sensitive to the students' backgrounds, health referrals to meet the physical needs of students and their families, communicating with parents in their own language, and offering extracurricular and career guidance programs to help students succeed in school and in their communities.

10. Research and develop a newcomer program to help orient immigrant students and their families to the school and its programs.

SOURCE: Adapted from Northwest Regional Educational Laboratory (2002).

#78: USING ENGLISH EFFECTIVELY WITH ENGLISH LANGUAGE LEARNERS

In classrooms of all English-speaking students, common norms of schooling—such as questions, lectures, and oral directions and feedback—prevail. However, such practices can be rethought when ELLs are present. There are simple techniques that mainstream teachers can integrate into daily instruction to increase the comprehension of language minority students.

Before Instruction

- Teach essential instruction and vocabulary words before assigning a task.
- Focus on five to ten core vocabulary words in each lesson.
- Sit students from similar cultural and linguistic groups together for peer support.
- If possible, have instructions translated into students' native languages and written on cards for them to refer to during the assignment.
- If possible, have visual images with English labels of the steps of the assignment or task.

Giving Instructions for Assignments

- Speak slowly and pause frequently.
- Avoid run-on sentences.
- Use butcher paper or an overhead projector to clarify oral directions.
- Use idiom-free language since not all students will understand expressions such as, "We had to twist her arm to participate."
- Emphasize key words in your speech, such as, "Get your paper and pencils. Turn to page 54 in your textbooks. We will solve problems one through five on page 54."

During an Assignment

- Use small-group activities to decrease isolation and increase participation.
- Use multimodal teaching processes as described in Chapter 2.
- Use visuals.
- Have one or more other students model doing the assignment first.
- Relate content to students' background cultural knowledge as much as possible. For example, the teacher can compare food, climate, clothing, holidays, or jobs in various locations.

- Increase wait time when asking a question.
- Ask only one question at a time,
- Avoid gestures, such as pointing, that may be considered culturally inappropriate.

At the End of an Assignment

- Ask for a brief oral or written summary of what was learned.
- Ask for opinions about the assignment.
- Have students show what was completed.
- Determine whether students met the instructional goals. If not, plan for tutoring or additional practice, or seek the services of a school or district ESL specialist.

#79: GEOMETRIC COLLABORATION

The strategic use of resources, limited language, peer learning, and charting can effectively introduce students to geometric concepts. To begin, organize students into pairs or small groups. Provide each group with textbooks, encyclopedias, or other materials that address the following common geometric figures. Adapt, copy, and distribute the form in Figure 4.3A.

Figure 4.3A   Geometric Shapes

Vocabulary	Written Definition	Drawing	Classroom Example
Line			
Ray			
Point			
Circle			
Degree			
Diameter			
Radius			
Arc			

Other terms for geometric figures can be added. Additionally, the figure can be adapted to include formulas for finding volume, perimeter, and circumference (see Figure 4.3B).

Figure 4.3B   Geometric Figures

Vocabulary	What is it?	What does it look like?	How do you find it?
Cube			
Cylinder			
Pyramid			
Rectangular prism			
Triangular prism			

#80: COLLABORATIVE NOTE TAKING

Students' class notes often reveal what they learned and did not learn during a lesson. For some students, note taking is distracting and confusing and, ultimately, unhelpful in preparing for tests. Such skills, however, can be improved when practiced collaboratively.

Ask your class to take notes during a lecture. For early grades—perhaps Grades 3, 4, and 5—the lecture should be brief (under six minutes) and clearly structured. Afterward, divide students into small, collaborative groups. Provide time for the groups to discuss the lecture and to identify its key points and important examples or supporting details. After their discussions, ask students to add new information to their notes. Next, ask questions of the small groups, and let them respond with a collective response. Later, encourage all students to use their collaborative notes for studying for tests or other class assignments (Schumm, Vaughn, & Sobol, 1997, p. 170).

A good way to structure a note-taking lesson is to identify several key points, which are outlined or bulleted on the whiteboard. These points can be the framework of student notes. Many teachers have students make small folded eight-page booklets from a piece of plain copy paper. Each bullet goes on one page of the booklet, with students writing their own notes or illustrations below the headings on each page. A simple example is shown in Figure 4.4 below.

Figure 4.4 Seven Point Lesson on Cells

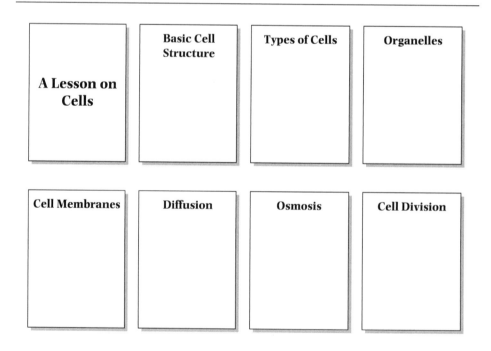

#81: TEACHING STANDARD ENGLISH IN THE MULTICULTURAL CLASSROOM

Many students speak dialects that differ from standard English. In the classroom, nonstandard English speakers should be encouraged to retain the language of their home, community, and peers while at the same time acquiring the language of education. Teachers can teach standard English with cultural sensitivity and ensure that students are successful with both languages. Figure 4.5 develops an awareness of language varieties and asks students to recognize and contrast the features of two linguistic systems.

Figure 4.5 Varieties of Language

Pronuciation

In the community	At school

Grammar Differences

In the community	At school

Vocabulary Terms

In the community	At school

Situation or Event

In the community	At school

#82: HIGH-PERFORMING TEACHERS OF HIGH-POVERTY STUDENTS

Haberman (1995) has identified the core behaviors of exemplary teachers of poor and disadvantaged students. In his 30 years of research, Haberman asserted that school reforms take hold only when they are supported by a system of pedagogy that is practiced schoolwide. He describes the characteristics of "star teachers" who have what it takes to help students succeed:

1. Star teachers are avid problem solvers. They seek to engage every student in learning—gifted, overlooked, academically challenged, or underserved (Haberman, 1995, pp. 21–28).

2. Star teachers go beyond the traditional textbook by scanning current school, community, and world events and using such topics to capture student interest. They model a contagious love of learning (pp. 29–41).

3. Star teachers use active learning processes and explain what they are doing and why. They point out the broad generalizations and concepts that undergird and connect daily lessons (pp. 41–48).

4. Star teachers assume responsibility for all students and do not attribute academic underachievement to shortcomings in the students themselves, the schools, or society (pp. 48–54).

5. Star teachers establish close and supportive relationships with students, not to satisfy their needs or preferences but to connect learning in ways that are meaningful for those they teach (pp. 54–60).

6. Star teachers address bureaucratic demands by prioritizing what is necessary and what may be optional. They grow adept at clerical tasks and record keeping, attend important meetings (and forgo others), and learn how to advocate for students outside the classroom (pp. 60–68).

7. Star teachers acknowledge their individual fallibility. They know they make mistakes, admit them, and work to correct and prevent them (pp. 68–71).

8. Star teachers have emotional and physical stamina fueled by an inherent enthusiasm for what they do. Such qualities prevent burnout and keep them engaged in the dailyness of teaching (pp. 71–73).

9. Star teachers have strong organizational and management skills, evident when using complex instructional methods, such as project-based learning, and when connecting the classroom with real-world experiences (pp. 73–76).

10. Star teachers believe that success is derived from effort rather than chance or talent and communicate this belief to students (pp. 76–78).

11. Star teachers distinguish between giving directions and providing instruction. They see teaching as interacting with students, not just giving explanations and expecting students independently to follow directions. They convey that the students and teacher are on the same side, the learning side, and that they are not pitted against each other (pp. 79–82).

12. Star teachers communicate that students are valuable members of a learning community and that, without them, the group would not be complete. Instead of using coercion, such teachers create safe havens and demonstrate respect by creating an inclusive classroom climate (pp. 83–86).

#83: REDUCING PREJUDICE BY INCREASING CRITICAL THINKING

Students can learn critical thinking skills that counteract prejudicial tendencies. Bias often emerges when students use faulty reasoning, such as overgeneralizing and not following thoughts to their logical conclusion. Cotton (1993, p. 6), in her work on fostering intercultural harmony, suggests that students can practice the following thinking skills as an antidote to bias and stereotyping.

Intellectual Curiosity

Seek answers to a wide variety of questions and problems. Consider the causes and explanations of events by asking who, what, why, when, and where.

Objectivity

Rely on evidence and valid arguments when making a decision.

Open-Mindedness

Consider numerous perspectives and beliefs as being simultaneously true.

Flexibility

Be willing to change your mind. Avoid rigid and dogmatic attitudes.

Healthy Skepticism

Be willing to reject a hypothesis until adequate evidence is available.

Intellectual Honesty

Accept a statement as true when the evidence warrants, even though it conflicts with a previously held belief.

Being Systematic

Follow a line of thinking to its logical conclusion. Stay on track when confronted by tangents or topics that are irrelevant.

Persistence

Pursue evidence and arguments to support a point of view.

Decisiveness

Be willing to arrive at a conclusion when there is adequate evidence.

Respecting Other Viewpoints

Listen respectfully to other viewpoints and be willing to admit if you are wrong, and another's ideas seem correct.

#84: MULTICULTURAL MATH

Math is often presented as empirical and objective, devoid of cultural content. As a collection of logical, verifiable processes, math is a universal language. However, when viewed through cultural and social systems, it becomes evident that there are different ways of perceiving the world mathematically. A few suggestions for integrating multiculturalism into math instruction follow.

1. Address the evolution of mathematical vocabulary. Some examples to consider include the Arabic origin of the word algebra, the Babylonian concept of sexagesimal numerals yielding hours and minutes, and the Hindu concept of zero.

2. Consider different approaches to classification systems. For example, the Cree and Ojibwa tribes classify plants and animals according to their function rather than using the Western system that is based on structure.

3. Use a variety of counting and measurement tools. For example, training with the Japanese abacus can assist students in transferring concepts to paper and pencil computations. Coast Salish tribes in the northwestern United States had a measurement that extended from the thumb to the middle fingertip with the forgers outstretched. Students can learn to estimate with this form of measurement and then convert it into English and metric forms.

4. The concepts of fractions, ratio, and proportion can be reinforced by making recipes from other cultures and by calculating currencies from other countries.

5. Patterning and symmetry can be studied in the art and architecture of many cultures.

6. Maps of different countries can be used to teach distance and proportion, while their calendars can show different ways of tracking time.

7. Invite guest speakers to the classroom to talk about how they use mathematics in daily life. For example, relatives and community members introduced one sixth grade class in the Southwest to the use of measurement, calculation, and fractions in the construction business.

8. *The World Almanac for Kids* (World Almanac, 2008; available in print and online at www.worldalmanacforkids.com) can serve as an excellent resource for percentages, statistical data, and graphing.

9. Students and guest speakers can teach one another multicultural games that use mathematical concepts.

#85: MULTICULTURAL LITERATURE

Multicultural literature can be used in the classroom to accomplish several important goals. Three include increasing the achievement of minority students, raising cultural awareness, and providing enrichment for all students. Much multicultural literature addresses the issue of identity and the interplay between defining ourselves through our differences from and commonalities with others. Since identity development is a primary task of adolescence, the following thematically organized literary suggestions target adolescents and support their efforts with identity formation (Brown & Stephens, 1998, pp. 35–100).

Connecting the Past With the Present

The book *The Diary of a Young Girl* by Anne Frank can be used to inspire memoir writing among immigrant (and all other) students. Discussions and writing assignments can address taking refuge, overcoming obstacles, lack of schooling, and longing for peace and stability.

Journeys

Selected books can be assigned to small groups of students who consider how journeys are portrayed and experienced by various literary characters. Such texts might include *Dogsong* by Gary Paulsen about an Alaskan Native boy's path to manhood; *Journey of the Sparrows* by Fran Leeper Buss about a family forced to flee El Salvador; and *Journey to Topaz* by Yoshiko Uchida about the internment of Japanese Americans during World War II.

Overcoming Obstacles

Persistence, effort, and positive attitudes are usually necessary ingredients for any success in life. Students can read one or more of the following books for inspiration to continue trying when the going gets tough: *Alicia: My Story* by Alicia Appleman-Jurman talks about surviving the Holocaust; *Winning* by Robin Brancato is about a star football player who becomes paralyzed after a tackle on the field; *Silver Rights* by Constance Curry recounts the desegregation of an all-white school in the South; and *The Story of My Life* by Helen Keller shows heroic efforts to live with deafness and blindness.

Writing One's Life

Rio Grande Stories by Carolyn Meyer demonstrates how students and teachers can successfully publish a book. A multicultural seventh grade class in New Mexico researched their own heritages and wrote about how their communities live along the Rio Grande. The book features the writing of Native American, Hispanic, African American, Anglo, and Jewish students and is an impressive model of how students can teach others about their cultures.

SUGGESTIONS FOR FURTHER INFORMATION ABOUT TEACHING DIVERSE STUDENTS

Adams, C. M., & Pierce, R. L. (2006). *Differentiating instruction: A practical guide to tiered lessons in the elementary grades*. Waco, TX: Prufrock Press.

> Differentiation is an important topic in education. As Adams and Pierce (2006) state, "At a time when many school systems around the world have embraced the inclusionary model to serve a diverse student body, it is vital that [classroom teachers] have the necessary tools to teach in the inclusionary classroom" (p. 1). The first half of the book describes the model on which the book is based and provides a tiered lesson example, template, and resources. The second half of the book provides examples of individual lessons and mini-units.

Banks, J., & Banks, C. (Eds.). (2006). *Multicultural education: Issues and perspectives* (6th ed.). New York: John Wiley.

> This classic in the field of multicultural education introduces educators to issues of race, class, gender, language and religious diversity, and exceptionality, and discusses the influence of such variables on student learning. Leading scholars define terms, present research, and address debates and controversies in the field. Topics include the evolution and characteristics of multicultural education, school and curricular reform, the limitations of color-blindness in the classroom, and numerous aspects of diversity. Also highlighted are classroom practices that successfully educate students from numerous backgrounds. This book is a must-read for anyone who wants a broad grounding in multicultural education, its goals, challenges, and promises.

Center for Research on Education, Diversity & Excellence (CREDE). *The five standards for effective pedagogy*. Available at http://www-gse.berkeley.edu/research/crede/standards/standards.html

> This Web site shows five standards for effective pedagogy of diverse students. CREDE researchers developed the standards and instructional strategies by analyzing the studies of educational researchers who worked with students at risk for educational failure due to cultural, language, racial, geographic, or economic factors. CREDE describes the standards and practices as effective with both majority and minority students in K–16 classrooms across subject areas, curricula, cultures, and language groups. A sample standard is "Joint productive activity." Two related practices are (1) designing instructional activities where students work together to complete a product, and (2) organizing student groups in diverse ways, such as by friendships, languages, interests, and mixed abilities. There is something for every teacher in these standards and strategies.

Haberman, M. (2004). *Star teachers: The ideology and best practice of effective teachers of diverse children and youth in poverty.* Houston, TX: Haberman Educational Foundation.

Drawing on his decades of research on educators who are effective with children of poverty, Martin Haberman provides a detailed description of the qualities and behaviors of those he identifies as "star teachers." He identifies: the pedagogy of poverty versus that of good teaching; the research base used to develop the "star teacher" typology; beliefs of star teachers; and functions of stars which can (or cannot) be assessed in interviews.

Ovando, C., Collier, V., & Combs, M. C. (2003). *Bilingual and ESL classrooms: Teaching in multicultural contexts.* Boston: McGraw-Hill.

Since most teachers have little or no training in working with ELLs in the classroom, this book is a worthy addition to any personal or professional library. The authors describe the brief history of bilingual education, untangle the numerous controversies surrounding this field, and give teachers needed guidance in teaching language minority students in the classroom. The scope of the book is broad and considers student demographic data, language policy and programs, effective classroom practices for ESL and mainstream teachers, the role of culture in learning, teaching and assessing a variety of disciplines, and school and community collaboration.

5

Assessing Student Performance

During the last two decades, the limitations of multiple-choice, matching, and true-or-false tests have caused educators to develop assessment alternatives. In classrooms across the country, teachers now use journals, presentations, portfolios, essays, and rubrics to assess student learning. More than ever before, assessment is regarded as an integrated component of the instructional process rather than an end-of-unit activity. This dissolution of the boundaries between teaching and assessing reflects broader educational shifts. Students are no longer perceived as passive recipients of information. They are active participants in their learning and, in many cases, are called on to demonstrate what they know.

As with any other aspect of education, assessment is a complex issue and one that evokes considerable debate. Rather than focus on controversies about standardized testing, this chapter maintains that data gathered from numerous sources can improve learning and teaching. Recent research, in fact, shows that new assessment procedures and varied uses of assessment data positively influence student learning (Black & Wiliam, 1998; DuFour, 2000; Educational Research Service, 2001; Massell, 2000; Marzano, 2006; Schmoker, 2001; Stiggins, 1994; U.S. Department of Education, 1997b; Wormelli, 2006).

For example, when teachers review individual student and whole-group responses to state level tests, they can specify the skills that were learned and those that require additional attention. Such awareness can be acted on to support students who might otherwise fall behind and to advance those who possess a thorough grasp of the content. Likewise, teachers report that classroom performance assessments often lead to meaningful changes in instruction and improved student motivation and achievement. (Black & Wiliam, 1998; Marzano, 2006; Stiggins, 1994, 2000; U.S. Department of Education, 1997b; Wiggins, 2000; Wiggins & McTighe, 1998). Some also claim that performance measures more equitably assess the performance of ethnic minority and language minority students (North Central Regional Educational Laboratory, 1997).

In the literature on assessment, there are conflicting terms, purposes, and processes. This chapter establishes a common frame of reference by defining concepts, clarifying the purposes of assessment, and describing 15 strategies. The concept of assessment used in this book is broader than that of assigning grades to students, and is instead perceived as an ongoing reflective process that involves collecting, synthesizing, and interpreting information about students' learning and teachers' teaching. It is important, also, to consider that classroom assessment serves several key purposes. These are as follows:

- To gather data about students' background knowledge
- To monitor learning
- To give students feedback during and after instruction
- To promote growth
- To recognize accomplishment
- To evaluate achievement
- To inform parents and the broader community about student learning
- To improve instruction
- To modify a program

It is helpful to be clear about the purposes of assessment, since all purposes are not necessarily compatible with one another. Emphasis on one purpose, such as end-of-the-term evaluative assessments, may not necessarily lead to enhanced pedagogy. It is unlikely that any one assessment will serve all purposes well. What is important is to match assessment purposes with the appropriate tasks. In general, effective classroom practices require a blend of three types of assessment: diagnostic, formative, and summative. These and other terms are defined below.

DEFINING ASSESSMENT TERMS

The field of assessment is replete with disagreements about the meaning of terms. Since there are literally no universally accepted definitions, those that follow have been culled and distilled from many sources. Just as these definitions serve as a starting point for this chapter, it is important when teachers discuss assessment in their schools that they define the terms they discuss.

Alternative assessment. This broad concept refers to any type of assessment in which students create responses to questions instead of responding to a prepared list of responses such as in multiple-choice, true-false, or matching questions. Sample alternative assessments include short-answer questions, essays, performances, oral presentations, and portfolios.

Assessment. Assessment is the process of quantifying, describing, gathering data, or giving feedback to others about what a learner knows and can do. Assessment results in identifying instructional practices that could be improved and supplying different resources for students. Various methods can be used to obtain information about student learning to guide decisions and actions. Some include observations, interviews, projects, tests, performances, and portfolios.

Authentic assessment. Authentic assessment is the process of gathering evidence or documenting a student's learning in ways that resemble real life, such as a driving test, a presentation, or addressing a community problem.

Diagnostic assessment. Diagnostic assessment typically occurs at the beginning of a unit of study or term. It involves identifying prior knowledge, using such strategies as those in Chapter 1, and is used to identify student difficulties, strengths, and interests and to make informed decisions about where to focus instruction.

Evaluation. Evaluation is the process of interpreting and making judgments about the quality, value, or worth of a response, product, or performance. Such judgments are usually based on established criteria.

Formative assessment. Formative assessment occurs frequently during teaching and learning. It provides ongoing diagnostic information to teachers about instructional effectiveness and to students about the status of their learning. Formative assessment occurs when teachers and students reflect on learning, give feedback, practice to improve skills, set goals, and make adjustments to teaching and learning.

Performance assessment. Performance assessments contrast with true-or-false and multiple-choice tasks by asking students to construct responses, create products, or perform demonstrations to provide evidence of what they know and can do.

Portfolio. A portfolio is a purposeful collection of products and criteria that demonstrate students' growth in knowledge and skill over time.

Reporting. Reporting consists of sharing information about student learning and often consists of evaluative judgments.

Rubric. A rubric is a set of scoring criteria used to guide and evaluate student work. Rubrics provide descriptive levels for performance, such as exemplary, competent, or novice.

Summative assessment. Summative assessment typically occurs at the end of a chapter, unit, course, grade level, or series of courses. It provides feedback to students, parents, and higher-education institutions about progress and achievement. Summative assessment typically leads to a status report on a student's degree of proficiency, and judgments are made according to established criteria. It is often used by others to make decisions about appropriate placement and helps students decide about further study. It is a snapshot of student achievement at a given time.

WHAT DOES THE RESEARCH SAY ABOUT USING ASSESSMENT TO IMPROVE TEACHING AND LEARNING?

Assessment is most beneficial when it is a natural, integrated part of the instructional cycle. As this brief literature review shows, well-conceived assessment can improve students' content knowledge and skills and simultaneously develop new roles for teachers and students alike. In response to the standards movement, approaches to streamlining the content demand of standards are also under way.

Because of the high-stakes nature of standardized tests, teachers often plan for assessment just as they do for instruction. In fact, many educational researchers suggest that teachers plan backward (Downs & Strand, 2006; Hibbard & Yakimowski, 1997; Wiggins & McTighe, 1998). To do so, teachers first identify the results they want to attain, then determine the forms of evidence that show whether results were achieved, and then move on to planning classroom learning experiences. Even before this cycle begins, it is helpful for teachers to base their instructional ideas on knowing their students' needs. This requires either formal or informal diagnostic forms of assessment to determine students' existing levels of knowledge (Bransford, Brown, & Cocking, 1999) which the first chapter of this books addresses. Before instruction begins, then, research suggests that teachers diagnose the extent of their students' knowledge and skills, then specify the outcomes they want to achieve and plan engaging ways to teach and meaningful ways to assess whether learning has occurred.

Among the many ideal "shoulds" placed upon teachers, much has been learned to guide assessment decisions and approaches for classroom consumption. Effective assessment practices are those that are closely aligned with curricular goals, collect student data over time, and, in some cases, span the K–12 years, include active student participation, sample a range of skills and competencies, are diverse and varied in their approaches, and are teacher designed (Marzano, 2003, 2006; Organization for Economic Cooperation and Development, 2005; U.S. Department of Education, 1997). Many studies also emphasize the power of formative assessment, since it plays an important role in shaping teaching and learning (Black & Wiliam, 1998; Daily, 2007; Marzano, 2003, 2006; Wiggins & McTighe, 1998).

THE POWER OF PERFORMANCE ASSESSMENT

Recent research has highlighted that performance assessment is particularly effective. It has been shown capable of positively altering classrooms for the better in four key ways: curriculum development, instruction, teacher roles, and student roles. These benefits are explained below.

Using portfolios as assessment tools has demonstrated a positive impact on the content of classroom curriculum. In some cases, portfolios influence what is taught by promoting depth rather than breadth of content coverage (U.S. Department of Education, 1997; Wininger & Norman, 2005). Students benefit by studying key concepts in and forgoing the all-too-frequent survey approach evident in many texts.

Scoring rubrics, another performance assessment measure, can clearly communicate what students are to learn and how well they are to learn it. When developed and explained prior to beginning work, such rubrics increase students' awareness of expectations and provide a frame of reference for judging their own work as well as that of their peers. An added benefit of rubrics is that student complaints about grades decrease when the criteria are clarified (U.S. Department of Education, 1997). There are benefits as well for teachers. Scoring rubrics allow teachers to easily identify students who struggle with content or skills. By acting on this increased awareness of achievement targets, teachers can help students meet expectations. For example, student failure rates were diminished when their teachers realized they needed increased study time and more assistance with math (Feldman & Tung, 2001).

Reducing the reliance on textbook-based assignments and tests changes the nature of instruction, too. When teachers assign performance-based tasks, students are typically required to use writing, content knowledge, and problem solving in their assessment activities (Harlan, 2003; U.S. Department of Education, 1997). Increased opportunities for students to use writing across the curriculum have yielded gains in students' writing skills. Similarly, performance tasks foster analytic thinking. This is because students must actively seek, structure, and communicate information to others and, in so doing, use a wide variety of thinking and language skills.

Increased use of formative types of assessment has been linked with significant achievement gains. In a review of 250 studies, Black and Wiliam (1998) and Marazno's (2006) later research found that formative assessment, often simply in the form of advice or feedback, benefited students at all ability levels, while grading did not result in improved work. Marzano (2003) notes that feedback should be timely and offered multiple times throughout the length of the class or school year.

Another instructional change brought about by performance assessment is increased collaboration among students (Feldman & Tung, 2001; Seidel, 1991; U.S. Department of Education, 1997). Presentations, exhibits, or experiments are often conducted by small groups of students. Additionally, the use of rubrics increases opportunities for peer assessment, since students know the targets for their learning and can self-assess or give advice to classmates.

Teacher roles have also transformed with performance assessment. Teachers become more reflective about their practices (Feldman & Tung, 2001; Harlan, 2003), and collaboration with colleagues increases. This occurs when teachers seek out peers to discuss details about performance assessment and to analyze portfolios that span multiple grades, levels, or subjects. Additionally, the U.S. Department of Education (1997) found that teacher creativity was enhanced through efforts to assign multiple forms of performance assessment.

Classroom assessment, and especially the use of performance-based measures, can make a critical difference in student learning (Black & Wiliam, 1998; Organization for Economic Cooperation and Development, 2005; Ulmer, 2001; U.S. Department of Education, 1997). Students have frequently exhibited a greater motivation when working on performance tasks and portfolio assignments than with traditional types of textbook-based assignments. Both teachers and students attributed this engagement to the sustained attention and effort such assignments necessitated. Likewise, students have demonstrated good research and presentation skills with project-based forms of assessment.

Many teachers ask students to participate in establishing assessment criteria and to self-assess their work. Student learning has benefited from this active participation (Pike, 1995; Seidel, 1991). Furthermore, when students are involved in their own assessment, they have opportunities to reflect on the quality of their learning. They become responsible for determining what and how they are learning and to consider their depth of content knowledge. Self-assessment, whether through journals or portfolios, helps students internalize academic goals, think critically, and become independent learners (Davison & Pearce, 1992).

In addition to determining student academic achievement, assessment can be directed towards capturing the nonacademic intangibles in the classroom (Lee, Harrison, & Black, 2004; Nelson, 2000). These often have to do with student behaviors and include behaviors such as a student's daily attendance, ability to engage socially in positive ways, and impulse control.

Frequently, teachers notice changes in students, but such changes are seldom measured. According to Nelson (2000), however, teachers can easily document five categories of nonacademic behavior: (a) attendance; (b) classroom participation, such as asking appropriate questions, engaging in small group tasks, and transferring learning to other situations; (c) attentiveness as demonstrated through on-task behavior; (d) social skills; and (e) classroom behaviors. Recording these five areas, as shown later in this chapter, can provide helpful information to students, parents, and colleagues. The areas serve as indicators of interpersonal and intrapersonal growth and can signal academic opportunities.

USING PERFORMANCE ASSESSMENT IN THE CLASSROOM

The brief research review above indicates that assessment can move from diagnosing student skills to reflecting on learning to deepening learning, and even include the intangibles that show a respect for learning. This shift occurs when teachers know the starting points of students, when they are explicit about what should be learned and how such learning should be expressed, when multiple assessment measures are used over time, and when students actively self-assess. The sixteen strategies that follow in this chapter attempt to dissolve traditional lines between learning and assessment and, in so doing, develop positive learning and reflecting or assessment cultures in classrooms.

The pages that follow address many aspects of assessment. These include planning for assessment, identifying assessment criteria, and techniques for taking standardized tests—a reality for nearly every student. Formative assessment processes are emphasized throughout. As a result, the reader will find sample learning logs, anecdotal records, observation guides, oral classroom assessment, and interviews. Last but not least, students are taught how to assess themselves. With an ability to direct and redirect their effort, students and teachers collaboratively can achieve a major goal of education—learning how to learn and how to improve one's learning.

#86: IT'S NOT BUSINESS AS USUAL: PLANNING FOR ASSESSMENT

To begin improving assessment, it is helpful to be intentional about how and why we teach the content we do and whether students will learn from our efforts. Some guiding questions answered at the outset of a new unit of study can ensure that learning is productive from start to finish.

Before Instruction

- Why do I include this content in what I teach?
- What will students know by the end of this unit?
- How does this content support the course's outcomes, the state's standards, or other goals?
- What do students already know about this material? How can I find out?
- How can I make my goals for learning clear?
- How should I inform students of the learning targets to be met?
- What evidence will show that students have learned the content?
- What instructional strategies do I plan to use?
- What adaptations might I need to make for individuals or groups?

During Instruction

- What advice can I give to help students?
- What kinds of feedback can students give each other?
- Who is stuck, and what can I do to jump-start their learning?
- How can I have students reflect on their thinking and modify it?
- How might students support each other in meeting the learning targets?

After Instruction

- How did students perform overall?
- How did they perform on specific objectives?
- How did different subgroups of students perform, such as those who are highly mobile or in a language minority?
- Why did they perform at that level?
- What can be done to improve their performance?
- How can I engage students in self-reflection about their learning?
- What remediation is needed and for whom?

#87: BEGINNING WITH THE END IN MIND

Planning for instruction is like planning a trip. The destination is identified first, the route and means of travel are determined, and the stops along the way are also mapped out. Of course, interesting and unplanned detours can occur, but people usually arrive at their desired destination somewhat on schedule and know how they got there. Planning instruction backward by specifying the desired results first, the acceptable evidence second, and the learning experiences third can help orient teachers and students to the journey ahead. The questions in Figure 5.1 guide the planning process.

Figure 5.1 Planning Worksheet

What important concepts or big picture ideas should students know?
(Examples: large concepts, theories, or principles, such as human rights in a democracy, how personal identity is addressed in literature, or the ability of the arts to mirror and lead culture)

What evidence will reveal that students understand? (Examples: projects, essays, quizzes, presentations, observations, and student self-assessment)

How will students know where they are headed? (Examples: rubrics, completed samples, and grading criteria)

What teaching and learning experiences will assist students in acquiring the targeted learnings? (Examples: sequence of instruction or learning activities)

_____

_____

_____

How will progress be gauged during instruction? (Examples: informal observations, teacher and student feedback, discussions)

_____

_____

_____

How will student learning be demonstrated? (Examples: performances and products)

_____

_____

_____

How will students self-assess? (Examples: debriefings, comparison of one's work against the rubric, journal entries)

_____

_____

_____

SOURCE: Adapted from G. Wiggins & I. McTighe (1996).

#88: TAKING STOCK: STUDENT SELF-ASSESSMENT

Students can learn to self-assess at young ages. Self-assessment helps students to internalize the learning goals, to identify the strengths and weaknesses of their work, and to manage their individual learning. Such processes can begin in the early grades. Figure 5.2A is an example of a primary-level rubric.

With older students, a summative self-assessment might look like the one in Figure 5.2B.

Figure 5.2A   Self-Rating for Younger Students

Name: _____   Date: _____

On this assignment, I think my work is:

4 = Super! This is my best work.

3 = Well done. I made good effort.

2 = OK. I could have done better. Ideas I have to improve this are:

1 = Not very good. I would like to redo this work. I need help with:

Figure 5.2B Self-Rating for Older Students

Name: _____

What key ideas did you learn from this unit?

_____

_____

_____

_____

_____

What did you learn about yourself from working on this assignment?

_____

_____

_____

_____

_____

What are the strengths of this assignment?

_____

_____

_____

_____

_____

What could be done to improve your work?

_____

_____

_____

_____

_____

Does this assignment meet the specified criteria? How or why not?

_____

_____

_____

_____

#89: COLLABORATIVE-ASSESSMENT CONFERENCES

Collaborative-assessment conferences, as developed by Seidel (1991), involve students and teachers in conversations about the quality of significant student work. Such conferences democratize the assessment process by giving those who will be assessed the opportunity to say what assessment should look like. Assessment conferences are usually conducted both before students start work on a major assignment and after they have completed it. The conferences are based on the assumption that serious student work deserves serious teacher and student response and attention.

First Conference: Establishing Assessment Criteria

Before embarking on an important assignment or project, teachers and students can collaboratively identify the criteria for assessing the completed work. During about 30 minutes of discussion, both content and skill criteria can be identified and refined. For example, students might suggest that their work exhibit a clear understanding of a concept and that their knowledge be displayed visually or extended into real-world applications. The acceptable levels of proficiency can also be identified. During the first collaborative assessment conference, teachers also might show samples of previous student work so the class can consider whether such models met the criteria and why or why not.

Second Conference: Assessing Student Work

The second collaborative-assessment conference is scheduled when assignments are due. Its intent is to showcase student work while also discussing how effectively the assignments met the pre-established criteria. Such conferences can be held individually, in small groups, or with the entire class. Guidelines follow for conducting this summative assessment process.

Discussion Guidelines

1. Ask students to explain their work, its quality, and what they learned.

2. In respectful, nonevaluative terms, describe the student's work.

3. Identify the most striking or noticeable features of the work. Ask whether the student has additional comments to make.

4. Ask questions about the work, and encourage classmates to do likewise.

5. Evaluate whether the work fulfills the pre-established criteria.

In closing the assessment conference, identify strengths evident in the assignment that could be extended to other work, and end on a positive note or with encouragement for future efforts.

#90: TEST-TAKING MATTERS

Standardized tests are likely here to stay. The skills they require can be taught and practiced by integrating them into common classroom assessments. Teachers can model how they would use each skill and in so doing demystify high-stakes test procedures while showing students how to do the following when taking a test:

1. Follow directions, including oral and written directions, and complex ones with multiple steps.

2. Respond to prompts by understanding what key terms mean, such as summarize, give an example, or show your work.

3. Practice using a variety of test formats.

4. Use answer sheets to find and mark the answer choices appropriately.

5. Manage time effectively by skipping difficult items to return to them later, allotting time to different segments of a test, and avoiding rushing,

6. Consider each answer choice by scanning for quick answers, making a good guess, eliminating incorrect options, determining when correct answers are not given, and checking one's choice.

7. Predict answers before considering options.

8. Refer to a passage to search for an answer.

9. Use key words, numbers, or graphs to solve problems.

10. Compute carefully.

#91: TEST-TAKING RULES FOR STUDENTS

Be excited to show what you know and can do.

1. Plan your time and pace yourself.

2. Read carefully, and ask yourself questions about what you are reading.

3. Follow directions, follow directions, follow directions.

4. Estimate an answer before looking at options.

5. Skip hard questions and answer easy questions first.

6. Know when and how to guess-eliminate obviously wrong answers and choose from among the best.

7. For writing tests, organize thoughts first and write in complete sentences.

8. Check your answers.

9. Use positive self-talk to complete the test with your best effort.

#92: GETTING TO KNOW YOU: ENTRY INTERVIEWS

Teachers can establish baseline data about student knowledge at the beginning of a unit or term by using diagnostic forms of assessment. One approach is to briefly interview students about a particular discipline. Older students or instructional aides can conduct the interviews and record responses, or students can use the forms as surveys to complete. Reflecting on the completed data gives teachers insight into the beginning knowledge and attitudes of those they are about to teach. Here is an example of a form for an entry interview (Campbell, Campbell, & Dickinson, 1999, p. 328):

Student name: _____ Date: _____

Subject or class: _____

Interviewer name: _____

1. Is there someone you know well who has a strong interest in this subject or topic?

2. If so, how do you know that person is interested in this topic?

3. What have you learned from that person about this topic? Or, where have you encountered this topic before?

4. What are one or two things you know about this topic?

5. What is one thing you would like to learn?

6. How do you think you could use this information in school? Outside of school?

7. How do you learn best? What could the teacher do to make this topic interesting?

#93: SAYING GOODBYE: EXIT INTERVIEWS

In contrast to entry interviews, exit interviews ask teachers and students to reflect on what was learned, how it was learned, and what might be next. A sample exit interview form follows (Campbell, Campbell, & Dickinson, 1999, p. 309).

Student name: _____ Date: _____

Subject or class: _____

Interviewer name: _____

1. Reflect on your earliest work in this class or on this topic. What are two or three key ideas you learned?

2. What did you learn that was new to you?

3. What did you most enjoy about the unit or course?

4. What problems did you encounter during the unit?

5. What did you learn about yourself as a learner from this class?

6. How can you use the information gained from this experience?

7. What grade do you think you deserve and why?

8. How have you changed because of this new knowledge?

9. What would like to learn next?

10. How would you get started?

#94: TAKING NOTE WITH ANECDOTAL RECORDS

Anecdotal records are brief notes that describe significant behaviors during observations. When they are collected and reviewed over time, they help teachers perceive patterns of learning and behavior, make instructional decisions, and give students feedback. There are many ways to organize this type of formative assessment. Some teachers make generic grids that are filed in notebooks alphabetically by student names. Some use notebooks for each subject area, others use note cards that are filed, and some use Post-it notes that are later added to a student's file. A sample anecdotal record is in Figure 5.3.

Figure 5.3 Anecdotal Record of Significant Behavior

Student name: Deloria

Subject: Fifth-grade math

1/12 Teacher Observation: After students were asked to plan a trip budget, Deloria looked out the window, sharpened her pencil, and asked to go to the bathroom. When she returned, she participated in making a draft budget.

1/16 Teacher Observation: Deloria spent the first few minutes of class asking for supplies and getting organized. She completed most problems individually.

1/24 Teacher Observation: Deloria had difficulty getting started during the first 10 minutes of class today but seemed to benefit from my restating the directions to her.

1/2 Recommendation: Assist Deloria with being prepared to start tasks on time.

SOURCE: Adapted from K. Pike & S. Salend (1995).

#95: MAKING RUBRICS

Rubrics are evaluative tools that describe the components of an assignment and levels for performance, such as novice, practitioner, and expert. They provide clear information to students and others about performance expectations and when students can assist in their development by suggesting the indicators of a quality performance. Establishing the contents of a rubric requires analysis of the specific material to be assessed and what responses might look like. Students can be involved in determining the characteristics of work at various levels of quality. The following guide assists in determining what student responses might look like at different score levels:

What would best-quality responses look like? List the characteristics below.

_____

_____

_____

_____

_____

_____

How many levels of performance are anticipated (3, 4, 5)? What would work look like at various levels? List the characteristics below.

5. _____

4. _____

3. _____

2. _____

1. _____

0. _____

Once a rubric is created, the individual students, their peers, and the teacher can all use the same form to provide feedback about the quality of any individual assignment. It is often interesting to see how opinions vary and why.

Figure 5.4 shows a sample rubric for assessing a piece of student writing. It includes spaces for the student to self-assess and to receive a classmate's and teacher's assessment.

Figure 5.4 Assessment of Student's Writing

Student name: _____

N = Novice—student's work shows emerging skills and knowledge.

A = Apprentice—student's work uses knowledge and skills adequately.

E = Exemplary—student's work is polished and error free.

Criterion	Novice	Apprentice	Exemplary	Self	Peer	Teacher
Writing conventions	Numerous errors in spelling, punctuation, or paragraphing.	A few errors in spelling, punctuation, or paragraphing. Some editing required.	Consistently correct spelling, punctuation, or paragraphing. Adds original touches.			
Sentence structure	Sentences are incomplete, rambling, choppy, or awkward.	Sentences have adequate structure but little variety.	Sentences flow, are varied and creative.			
Vocabulary	Limited vocabulary. Lack of imagery or examples.	Ordinary language is used and conveys message but without imagery.	Word choice is interesting, with vivid images and creative expression.			
Ideas and content	Lacks focus.	Clear and focused writing.	Clear and focused writing that is engaging.			

To assist teachers with developing rubrics for any subject area, the list below suggests evaluative descriptions of student work at four levels of quality. Teachers (and students) can decide how many levels are appropriate for assessing an assignment, and then select the scoring scales to insert into the blank classroom-made rubric form in Figure 5.5.

Generalized Scoring Scales for Classroom-Made Rubrics

Level 4

Shows in-depth knowledge of the subject.

Expresses ideas clearly and succinctly.

Discusses ideas in a highly logical manner.

Addresses all of the questions posed.

Shows complete preparation when responding.

Makes highly detailed response.

Describes concepts without errors.

Level 3

Shows good knowledge of the subject.

Expresses ideas adequately.

Discusses ideas in a logical manner.

Addresses all of the questions posed.

Shows adequate preparation when responding.

Misses few details when responding.

Demonstrates minor misconceptions when responding.

Level 2

Shows some knowledge of the subject.

Expresses ideas with some disorganization.

Shows some illogical thought in discussion.

Addresses most of the questions posed.

Shows some preparation when responding.

Includes some details when responding.

Demonstrates major misconceptions when responding.

Level 1

Shows very little knowledge of the subject.

Expresses ideas in a very disorganized manner.

Shows much illogical thought in discussion.

Addresses very few of the questions posed.

Shows little preparation when responding.

Misses most details when responding.

Demonstrates that conceptions are mostly in error.

Figure 5.5 Generic Rubric Criteria

Scale: Criteria:				

#96: ASSESSING ORALLY

Think alouds, or oral defenses, as Nunley (2000, p. 6) calls them, are brief student–teacher interactions in which students are asked to explain their thinking or learning during class time, Teachers can check in with each student at least once every two days by moving around the class and posing questions one-on-one. Such formative oral assessments short-circuit student misconceptions or confusion and prevent them from slipping through proverbial classroom cracks. Sample one-on-one assessment questions follow:

1. How would you rephrase my directions?

2. How will you start this task?

3. What is the next step you would take?

4. Tell me how you arrived at that decision.

5. Explain that idea.

6. How would you define that?

7. Can you explain this answer?

8. Compare this part of your work with this criterion on the rubric.

9. Can you give another example of that?

10. How could you improve your thinking about this?

#97: OBSERVATION LOGS

On a daily basis, teachers observe students' academic and behavioral interactions. Usually, such observations are informal and rarely documented. However, with intentional use, observations can yield important insights. Some teachers structure observations by setting aside a portion of a day for such activities or by planning to observe designated skills or specific students. Observations can also be unstructured by simply jotting down significant student events or behaviors. Teachers can develop generic observation guides that readily accommodate their goals. It is often helpful to make accompanying narrative comments (see Figure 5.6).

Figure 5.6 Observation Checklist

Class: _____   Date: _____

Ratings:

N = There is no evidence that student knows or uses the skill.

B = Student is beginning to use the skill.

P = Student is making progress in developing the skill.

C = Student displays competence.

Student Names	Target Skill	Target Skill	Narrative Comments
1.			
2.			
3.			
4.			
5.			

#98: CHECKING THEIR LISTS: STUDENT CHECKLISTS

Students can gauge their skill development against predetermined criteria displayed on simple checklists. When given the opportunity to do so, they can analyze, describe, and evaluate their learning experiences, successes, and challenges. The checklist in Figure 5.7 targets reading skills.

Figure 5.7 Student Self-Assessment of Reading Skills

Name: _____ Date: _____

Reading Skills	Never	Sometimes	Often
I enjoy reading.			
I ask myself questions when I read.			
I can summarize what I read.			
I take notes or highlight when I read.			

Reading Skills	Never	Sometimes	Often
I use other words, or the context, to understand a new word.			
I make graphic organizers of what I read.			
I connect what I read to my life.			
I write about what I read.			

#99: LEARNING LOGS

Learning logs can accomplish several learning and assessment goals. They encourage students to write and reason simultaneously, and they reflect growth over time. They can serve as diagnostic, formative, or summative assessment tools. Those students who have difficulty writing can maintain an audio log by recording their reflections. Since the quality of students' writing can be enhanced with framed prompts, several are offered below:

1. Explain what you liked about the lesson today.

2. Define a key concept in your own words.

3. Write about what you didn't like today.

4. Explain how you arrived at a solution to the problem.

5. At the end of class today, write about what you learned, what was confusing, and what help you'd like to receive.

6. Defend your opinion about today's topic.

7. Connect what we are studying with something in the news or in your life.

8. Describe how you would teach a concept to someone you know.

9. Identify ways to improve this learning experience.

10. Evaluate an assignment or project against the specified criteria and arrive at a defensible grade.

#100: ASSESSING NONTRADITIONAL RESULTS

At times, it is helpful to have data to report student improvement in areas other than grades. It can make a difference to students, parents, and administrators to be able to explain, for example, that a student's attendance has improved by 40 percent over last semester, that complaints from others about behavior problems have decreased by one third in the last month, or that the student is asking at least three worthwhile questions weekly. Figure 5.8 is adapted from the work of Nelson (2000), who recommends that a teacher track a student's behavior for two days a week only (in this figure, Tuesdays and Thursdays), so that attention isn't diverted from others in the classroom.

Figure 5.8 Nontraditional Assessment of Student

Student: _____ Month: _____							
Absences: _____ Referrals: _____ Tardies: _____							
Social Behaviors	T	Th	T	Th	T	Th	T	Th
Negative (impulsive, disruptive, bullying, etc.)								
Positive (appropriate, supportive, helpful, etc.)								
Engagement								
Negative (apathetic, off task, uninterested, etc.)								
Positive (attentive, makes effort, asks questions, etc.)								
Reactions From Others								
Negative (complaints, infractions, avoidance, etc.)								
Positive (compliments, perceived as positive leader)								

SOURCE: From Linda Campbell, Bruce Campbell, & Dee Dickinson. *Teaching and Learning Through Multiple Intelligences*. 3rd Edition. Published by Allyn & Bacon, Boston, MA. Copyright © 2004 by Pearson Education. Adapted by permission of the publisher.

#101: SCHEDULING ASSESSMENT

Teachers typically spend a great deal of time planning a quarter-, trimester-, or semester-long curriculum. The same kind of planning can lead to the development of a comprehensive assessment calendar. Teachers can occasionally step back and reflect on the timing and types of assessment that are most appropriate for their curricular goals. The schedule in Figure 5.9 is suggested as one possible model and features diagnostic, formative, and summative forms of assessment. Each item could serve as one entry into a student portfolio to reveal growth over time through multiple measures.

Figure 5.9 Assessment Calendar

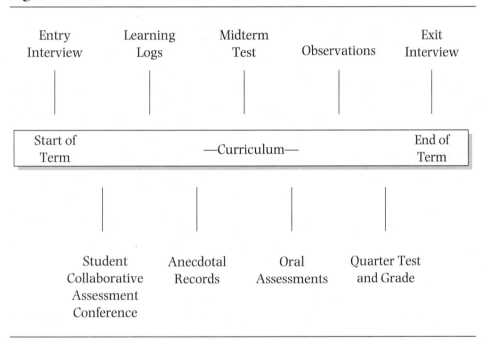

SOURCE: Adapted from L. Campbell, B. Campbell, & D. Dickinson (1999).

SUGGESTIONS FOR FURTHER INFORMATION ABOUT ASSESSMENT

Marzano, R. (2006). *Classroom assessment and grading that work.* Alexandria, VA: Association for Supervision and Curriculum Development.

This text, which is available in a downloadable format, provides an in-depth exploration of what Marzano calls "one of the most powerful weapons in a teacher's arsenal." An effective standards-based, formative assessment program can help to dramatically enhance student achievement throughout the K–12 system, Marzano says. Drawing from his own and others' research, the author provides answers to questions such as these:

- What are the characteristics of an effective assessment program?
- What types of assessment items and tasks are best suited to measuring student progress in mastering information, mental procedures, and psychomotor procedures?
- What types of scoring and final grading systems provide the most accurate portrayal of a student's progress along a continuum of learning?

Marzano, R. J., & Haystead, M. W. (2008). *Making standards useful in the classroom.* Alexandria, VA: Association for Supervision and Curriculum Development.

This book confronts common challenges teachers face with the standards-based movement. It begins by identifying the content requirements of current curriculum standards and shows teachers how to streamline the array of content objectives they are expected to teach and assess. Geared for educators at all grade levels, the book offers detailed scoring guides for the core subjects of math, language arts, science, social studies, as well as life skills.

Northwest Regional Educational Laboratory. (2007). *Toolkit98.* Available at http://www.nwrel.org/assessment/toolkit98.php

This Web site provides an overview of assessment helpful for individual teachers or as an inservice session.

Stiggins, R. (2005). *Student-involved classroom assessment* (4th ed.). Upper Saddle River, NJ: Prentice Hall.

This book describes how to conduct daily assessment and how to use assessment to benefit students. It offers practical information on developing a variety of assessment tools, ways to match learning goals with assessment methods, and how to communicate assessment results. Stiggins also emphasizes the well-being of students in an assessment culture by emphasizing the important role of student self-assessment. In this work, Stiggins continues to develop and express his philosophy that students should not be victimized by assessment but rather benefit from the process through active participation that eventually leads to internalized goals of high standards.

Tannenbaum, J. (1996). *Practical ideas on alternative assessment for ESL students.* Center for Applied Linguistics. Available at http://www.cal.org/resources/Digest/tannen01.html

This resource is helpful for those seeking practical ideas for assessing ESL students.

Uniserve. (2006). *Alternative strategies for science teaching and assessment.* Available at http://science.uniserve.edu.au/school/support/strategy.html

This website is especially appropriate for those interested in ways to assess learning in science.

Wiggins, G., & McTighe, J. (2005). *Understanding by design* (2nd ed.). Alexandria, VA: Association for Supervision and Curriculum Development.

Although it does not address assessment exclusively, this book explains backward curricular design that says teacher-designers should begin with the end in mind. Wiggins and McTighe maintain that before educators anywhere along the K–16 spectrum begin planning curriculum, they should consider (a) what they want students to learn and understand, (b) what forms of evidence could document whether such learning was attained, and (c) appropriate learning experiences and instruction. Performance assessments naturally emerge within the context of meaningful learning.

Wormelli, R. (2006). *Fair isn't always equal: Assessing and grading in the differentiated classroom.* Portland, ME: Stenhouse.

This book, which is written for middle and high school teachers, offers research and commonsense thinking for teachers and administrators wanting reliable and helpful information about assessment and grading. Wormelli covers the full assessment cycle in the classroom by addressing student readiness, learning outcomes, varied assessment strategies, and taking action after assessment. The author also tackles important and sometimes controversial issues, such as "What is mastery?" "What are the most important types of assessment?" "How should teachers grade students with special needs in inclusive classrooms?" Impressive in its approach to theory and research, the book is equally complete in its nitty-gritty details of the how-tos of grading and assessment.

6

Some Concluding Thoughts

When we walk through the hallways of schools in America, the complexity of teaching asserts itself. Observers find from quick visits in many classrooms a dizzying array of students all with pressing needs. There are those who are native to the local community and others new to the United States, those who have been at the school for two or more years and those who arrived yesterday or last week. Just as the students are diverse in their backgrounds and experiences, so too are the instructional techniques under way. In most classrooms, there are intricate webs of whole-group, small-group, and individualized instruction under way. It is readily apparent that some students appear engaged when they learn through listening and observation, while others gravitate toward hands-on activities, drawing, and physical movement. Some effortlessly engage in quick dialogue while others appear uncertain and struggle. A network of resource teachers, specialists, and classroom teachers discuss whom to help, when, and how. Teachers' conversations include lively discussions of state standards, assessment requirements, teachers' curricular interests, students' interests, community goals, and instructional strategies.

At the end of a school visit, impressions linger of the rich and daunting mix of student nationalities, languages, and academic levels, and of the packed curriculum that must be taught during a few short months. Education is a daily thousand-piece jigsaw puzzle. How does one begin to fit the pieces together?

We can start where this book began by learning about our students and their communities by considering what they know or think they know. When we engage students' background knowledge, we can meet our students where they are and identify new academic levels for them to reach. As described earlier, we can use backward planning, and in so doing, carefully articulate the outcomes students can attain. We can pick and choose any number of effective teaching techniques described in the pages of this book, and assess students' needs to flexibly adjust our approaches. We can vary the difficulty and pacing of our lessons, our texts, the types of questions we ask, the kinds of everyday connections made, and the assessments used so that every student experiences success. And, to accomplish all this or even any part of this, we need to be knowledgeable about what works in the classroom.

The complex demands of the classroom, let alone the mysteries of the human mind and its ability to learn and improve learning, require that teachers be lifelong students of learning. While we teach students important skills, knowledge, and attitudes, we can model what it means to be engaged learners ourselves. We can share with them our joys, challenges, and successes at understanding learning and the respect we have for research, reflection, and education itself. We can also appreciate that as the daily demands of teaching increase, so too has available research on what works. We are fortunate to work at a time when new forms of support are available to guide our efforts.

We all want thoughtful, engaged, and mindful students. We know that every student is unique and deserves the opportunity to learn, grow, and become all that is possible. The lofty ideals that drew us to education in the first place—improving lives one by one, class by class, year by year, so that our communities are better places to live and the future is bright with capable, caring, creative people—are all within our grasp. Such goals are realized when students are excited about learning. Excitement for learning is the result of excellent instruction.

This book taps the research on teaching and learning to put the tools of excellent instruction into the hands of teachers. By understanding the hows and whys of what works in classrooms, teachers and students are likely to experience greater success. We hope that our efforts support yours and that you agree that the 101 strategies here are worthy of being included in a mindful teacher's classroom repertoire.

References

Adams, C. & Pierce, R. (2003). Teaching by tiering. Retrieved June 13, 2008 from www.nsta.org/publications/news/story.aspx?id=48723

Adams, C., & Pierce, R. (2005). Using tiered lessons in mathematics. *Mathematics Teaching in the Middle School, 11*(3), 144–149.

Adams, C., & Pierce, R. (2006). *Differentiating instruction: A practical guide for tiering lessons in the elementary grades.* Waco, TX: Prufrock Press.

Aesop. (n.d.). *Fables.* Retrieved August 2, 2002, from http://www.aesopfables.com

Allington, R. L. (2001). *What really matters for struggling readers: Designing research-based programs.* New York: Longman.

American Association of School Administrators. (2001). *An educator's guide to schoolwide reform.* Retrieved April 30, 2008, from http://www.aasa.org/issues_and_insights/district_organization/Reform/index.htm

American Association of University Women Educational Foundation. (1992). *How schools shortchange girls.* New York: Marlowe.

American Association of University Women Educational Foundation. (1998). *Gender gaps: Where schools still fail our children.* Washington, DC: Author.

Anderson, J. (2007). *Encouraging girls in math and science.* Cambridge, Harvard Graduate School of Education. Retrieved April 30, 2008, from http://www.gse.harvard.edu/news_events/features/2007/11/21_star.html

Andreasen, N. C., O'Leary, D. S., Paradisio, S., Cizadlo, T., Arndt, S., Watkins, G., et al. (1999). The cerebellum plays a role in conscious episodic memory retrieval. *Human Brain Mapping, 8*(4), 226–234.

Aronson, E., Stephan, C., Sikes, J., Blaney, N., & Snapp, M. (1978). *The jigsaw classroom.* Thousand Oaks, CA: Sage Publications.

Arroyo, A., Rhoad, R., & Drew, P. (1999). Meeting diverse student needs in urban schools: Research-based recommendations for school personnel. *Preventing School Failure, 43*(4), 145–153.

Association for Supervision and Curriculum Development. (2000). *Before it's too late: Giving reading a last chance* (curriculum update). Alexandria, VA: Author.

Ball, D. (1993). With an eye on the mathematical horizon: Dilemmas of teaching elementary school mathematics. *Elementary School Journal, 93,* 373–397.

Banks, J., & Banks, C. (Eds.). (2006). Multicultural education: Issues and perspectives (6th ed.). New York: John Wiley.

Barnett, R., & Rivers, C. (2006). The boy crisis—Fact or myth? *Teachers College Record*. Retrieved February 22, 2008, from http://www.tcrecord.org/Content.asp?Content ID=12750

Barrell, I. (2001). Designing the invitational environment. In A. Costa (Ed.), *Developing minds: A resource book for teaching thinking* (3rd ed.) (pp. 106–110). Alexandria, VA: Association for Supervision and Curriculum Development.

Baum, S., Renzulli, S., & Hebert, T. (1995). The prism metaphor: A new paradigm for reversing underachievement. *Gifted Child Quarterly, 39*(4), 224–235.

Bauer, H. (1997). *High poverty, high performing: High hope.* Intercultural Development Research Association. Retrieved May 4, 2008, from http://www.starcenter.org/articles/highhope.html

Bazler, J., & Simonis, D. (1990). Are women out of the picture? *Science Teaches; 57*(9), 24–26.

Beck, I., & McKeown, M. (1981, Nov.–Dec.). Developing questions that promote comprehension: The story map. *Language Arts, 58,* 913–918.

Biemans, H., & Simons, P. (1996). A computer-assisted instructional strategy for promoting conceptual change. *Instructional Science, 24,* 157–176.

Bishop, J. (2006). *Success for boys: Helping boys achieve.* Retrieved February 24, 2008, from http://www.successforboys.edu.au/boys/

Black, P., & Wiliam, D. (1998). Inside the black box: Raising standards through classroom assessment. *Phi Delta Kappan, 80*(2), 139–159.

Bolin, L. (2005). A word is worth a thousand pictures. *Math Teacher Quarterly, 6* (1).

Bracey, G.W. (2006, November). *Separate but superior? A review of issues and data bearing on single-sex education* (ESPL-0611–211-EPRU). Tempe, AZ: Arizona State University, Education Policy Research University.

Bransford, J. D., Brown, A. L., & Cocking, R. R. (Eds.). (1999). *How people learn: Brain, mind, experience, and school.* Washington, DC: National Academy Press.

Bransford, J. D., Brown, A. L, & Cocking, R. R. (Eds.). (2000). *How people learn: Brain, mind, experience, and school.* (Expanded Ed.). Washington, DC: National Academy Press.

Bransford, J. D. & Donovan, S. M. (2005). *How students learn: History, mathematics, and science in the classroom.* Washington, DC: National Academies Press.

Brice, A., & Roseberry-McKibbin, C. (1999). Turning frustration into success for English language learners. *Educational Leadership, 56*(7), 53–55.

Brophy, J. (2000). *Teaching.* Geneva, Switzerland: International Academy of Education.

Brown J. E., & Stephens, E. C. (Eds.). (1998). *United in diversity: Using multicultural young adult literature in the classroom.* Urbana, Il. National Council of Teachers of English.

Brown, L. M., & Gilligan, C. (1992). *Meeting at the crossroads: Women's psychology and girls' development.* Cambridge, MA: Harvard University Press.

Bullock, L. D. (1997). Efficacy of gender and ethnic equity in science education curriculum for preservice teachers. *Journal of Research in Science Teaching, 34*(10), 1019–1038.

Campbell, L., & Campbell, B. (1999). *Multiple intelligences and student achievement: Success stories from six schools.* Alexandria, VA: Association for Supervision and Curriculum Development.

Campbell, L., Campbell, B., & Dickinson, D. (1999). *Teaching and learning through multiple intelligences.* Needham Heights, MA: Allyn & Bacon.

Campbell, L., Campbell, B., & Dickinson, D. (2004). *Teaching and learning through multiple intelligences* (3rd ed.). Boston: Allyn & Bacon.

Campbell, P. B., & Sanders, J. (1997). Uninformed but interested: Findings of a national survey on gender equity in preservice teacher education. *Journal of Teacher Education, 48*(1), 69–75.

Carey, S., & Gelman, R. (Eds.). (1991). *The epigenesis of mind: Essays on biology and cognition.* Hillsdale, NJ: Lawrence Erlbaum.

Carpenter, T., Fennema, E., & Franke, M. (1996). Cognitively guided instruction: A knowledge base for reform in primary mathematics instruction. *Elementary School Journal, 97*(1), 3–20.

Carpenter, T., & Fennema, F. (1992). Cognitively guided instruction: Building on the knowledge of students and teachers. *International Journal of Educational Research, 17,* 457–470.

Cawelti, G. (Ed.). (2004). *Handbook of research on improving student achievement* (2nd ed.). Arlington, VA: Educational Research Service.

Center for Public Education. (2008). *Minority students make gains on national assessment although achievement gaps remain.* Retrieved February 22, 2008, from http://www.centerforpubliceducation.org/site/c.kjJXJ5MPIwE/b.345

Center for Research on Education, Diversity & Excellence (CREDE). *The five standards for effective pedagogy.* Retrieved June 22, 2008 from http://www-gse.berkeley.edu/research/crede/standards/standards.html

Children's Hospital Boston. (2007). *A first glimpse at healthy brain and behavioral development.* Retrieved February 22, 2008, from http://www.childrenshospital.org/newsroom/Site1339/mainpagesS1339P1subleve1307.html

Christen, W. L., & Murphy, T. J. (1991). *Increasing comprehension by activating prior knowledge.* ERIC Digest #61. Bloomington, IN: ERIC Clearinghouse on Reading, English, and Communication. (ERIC Document Reproduction Service No. ED 328 885)

Coates, R. D. (1989). The regular education initiative and opinions of regular classroom teachers. *Journal of Learning Disabilities, 22,* 532–536.

Cohen, J. (2005). *Girls learning alone: Social transgression and a single-sex math classroom.* Paper presented at the annual meeting of the American Sociological Association, Marriott Hotel, Loews Philadelphia Hotel, Philadelphia, PA, August 12, 2005. Retrieved May 1, 2008, from http://www.allacademic.com/meta/p23034_index.html

Coley, R. (2001). *Differences in the gender gap: Comparisons across the radical/ethnic groups in education and work,* Princeton, NJ: Educational Testing Service.

Collicott, J. (1991). Implementing multi-level instruction: Strategies for classroom teachers. In G. L. Porter & D. Richter (Eds.), *Changing Canadian schools: Perspectives on disability and inclusion* (pp. 191–218). Toronto, Ontario: G. Allen Roeher Institute.

Cooney, S., & Bottoms, G. (2002). *Middle grades to high school: Mending a weak link.* Atlanta, GA: Southern Regional Education Board.

Corbett, H. D., & Wilson, B. L. (2000). *Students' perspectives on the Ninth Grade Academy of the Talent Development High Schools in Philadelphia: 1999–2000.* Philadelphia: Philadelphia Education Fund.

Cotton, K. (1993). *Fostering intercultural harmony.* Portland, OR: Northwest Regional Educational Laboratory. Retrieved May 2, 2008, from http://www.nwrel.org/scpd/sirs/8/topsyn7.html

Daggett, W., & Nussbaum, P. (2007). *How brain research relates to rigor, relevance and relationships.* Retrieved on January 5, 2008, from http://www.leadered.com/pdf/Brain%20Research%20White%20Paper.pdf

Daily, M. (2007). *Using formative assessment to improve teaching and learning.* Retrieved on January 5, 2008, from http://www.ncslma.org/2007Conference/Handouts/56-FormativeAssessment.ppt

Damasio, A. R., & Damasio, H. (1993). Brain and language. In *Mind and brain* (pp. 54–65). New York: W. H. Freeman.

Davey, B. (1983, October). Think aloud: Modeling the cognitive processes of reading comprehension. *Journal of Reading, 27,* 44–47.

Davison, D. M., & Pearce, D. L. (1992). The influence of writing activities on the mathematics learning of Native American students. *The Journal of Educational Issues of Language Minority Students, 10,* 147–157.

Diamond, B., & Moore, M. (1993). *Using multicultural literature to increase reading engagement and comprehension.* Retrieved May 5, 2008, from the Center for Multicultural Education, University of Washington, http://depts.washington.edu/centerme/mlp.htm

Diamond, M., & Hopson, J. (1998). *Magic trees of the mind: How to nurture your child's intelligence, creativity, and healthy emotions from birth through adolescence.* New York: Penguin.

Dochy, F. J., & Alexander, P. A. (1995). Mapping prior knowledge: A framework for discussion among researchers. *European Journal of Psychology of Education, 10*(3), 225–242.

Dolezal, S. E., Welsh, L. M., Pressley, M., & Vincent, M. M. (2003). How nine third-grade teachers motivate student academic engagement. *The Elementary School Journal, 103*(3), 239–267.

DomNwachukwu, C. S. (2005, Fall). Standards-based planning and teaching in a multicultural classroom. *Multicultural Education, 13,* 40–44.

Donovan, M. S., & Bransford, J. D. (Eds.). (2005). *How students learn: History, mathematics, and science in the classroom.* Washington, DC: The National Academies Press.

Downs, A., & Strand, P. (2006). Using assessment to improve the effectiveness of early childhood education. *Journal of Child and Family Studies, 15*(6), 671–680.

Dufour, R. (2000). Data put a face on shared vision. *Journal of Staff Development, 21*(1), 71–72.

Dunn, R., & Dunn, K. (1978). *Teaching students through their individual learning styles: A practical approach.* Boston: Allyn & Bacon.

Education for All Handicapped Children Act. (1975). Pub. L. No. 94–142.

Educational Development Corporation. (1999). *Women's Educational Equity Act: 1999 fact sheet on women's and girls' educational equity.* Newton, MA: Author.

Educational Research Service. (2001). *Student mobility.* Arlington, VA: Author.

Educational Research Service. (2004). *Helping students transition to high school.* Alexandria, VA: Author.

Educational Research Service. (2006). *Incorporating research-based teaching strategies.* Alexandria, VA: Author.

Educational Research Service. (2007a). *Educating boys.* Alexandria, VA: Author.

Educational Research Service. (2007b). *Elements of highly effective mathematics programs.* Alexandria, VA: Author.

Education Review Office. (2000). *Promoting boys' achievement.* Retrieved April 30, 2008, from http://www.ero.govt.nz/ero/publishing.nsf/Content/Promoting%20Boys'%20Achievement

Elbaum, B., Moody, S., Vaughn, S., Schumm, J., & Hughes, M. (1999). *The effects of instructional grouping format on the reading outcomes of students with disabilities: A meta-analytic review.* National Center for Learning Disabilities. Retrieved May 1, 2008, from http://www.ncld.org/content/view/522/

Ellis, A. K., & Fouts, J. T. (1997). *Research on educational innovations.* Larchmont, NY: Eye on Education.

Ellis, A. (2005). *Research on educational innovations.* Larchmont, NY: Eye on Education.

Ellison, C. M., Boykin, A. W., Towns, D. P., & Stokes, A. (2000). *Classroom cultural ecology: The dynamics of classroom life in schools serving low-income African-American children.* Washington, DC: Howard University. Retrieved January 27, 2008, from http://www.csos.jhu.edu/crespar/techReports/Report44.pdf

Feldman, J., & Tung, R. (2001, Summer). Using data-based inquiry and decision making to improve instruction. *ERS Spectrum, 19,* 10–19.

Fletcher, R. (2006). *Boy writers: Reclaiming their voices.* Portland, ME: Stenhouse.

Fountas, I., & Pinnell, G. (2001). *Guiding readers and writers: Teaching comprehension, genre, and content literacy.* New York: Heinemann.

Frasier, M., & Passow, A. (1994). *Toward a new paradigm for identifying talent potential* [Monograph 94112]. Storrs, CT: National Research Center on the Gifted and Talented.

Fuson, K. C., Kalchman, M., & Bransford, J. D. (2005). Mathematical understanding: An introduction. In M. Donovan & J. D. Bransford (Eds.), *How students learn: History, mathematics, and science in the classroom* (pp. 217–256). Washington, DC: The National Academies Press.

Gabel, D. (2004). Chapter 9: Science. In G. Cawelti (Ed.), *Handbook of research for improving student achievement* (3rd ed.) (pp. 202–225). Arlington, VA: Educational Research Service.

Gardner, H. (1983). *Frames of mind: The theory of multiple intelligences.* New York: Basic Books.

Gardner, H. (1985). *The mind's new science: A history of the cognitive revolution.* New York: Basic Books.

Gardner, H. (1991). *The unschooled mind: How children think and how schools should teach.* New York: Basic Books.

Gardner, H. (2000). *The disciplined mind: Beyond facts and standardized tests: The K–12 education that every child deserves.* New York: Penguin Books.

Gardner, H. (2003). *Multiple intelligences after 20 years.* Paper presented at the American Educational Research Association Conference. Chicago: Author.

Gay, G. (1989). Ethnic minorities and educational equality. In J. A. Banks & C. A. M. Banks (Eds.), *Multicultural education: Issues and perspectives* (pp. 167–188). Needham Heights, MA: Allyn & Bacon.

Gay, G. (2001). Educational equality for students of color. In J. A. Banks & C. A. M. Banks (Eds.), *Multicultural education: Issues and perspectives* (pp. 197–224). New York: John Wiley.

Gersten, R., & Clarke, B. S. (2007). *Effective strategies for teaching students with difficulties in mathematics* (Research Brief). Retrieved December 30, 2007, from htpp://www.nctm.org/uploadedFiles/Research_IssuesandNews/Briefs_andClips/research%20brief%2002%20%20Effective%20Strategies(1).pdf

Gersten, R., Baker, S., Marks, S., & Smith, S. (1999). *Effective instruction for learning disabled or at-risk English-language learners: An integrative synthesis of the empirical and professional knowledge bases.* National Center for Learning Disabilities. Retrieved April 30, 2008, from http://www.ncld.org/content/view/519/

Gilligan, C. (1982). *In a different voice: Psychological theory and women's development.* Cambridge, MA: Harvard University Press.

Glasser, W. (1990). The quality school. *Phi Delta Kappan, 71*(6), 424–435.

Glynn, C. (2001). *Learning on their feet: A sourcebook for kinesthetic learning across the curriculum.* Shoreham, VT: Discover Writing Press.

Goldstein, G., Haldane, D., & Mitchell, C. (1990). Sex differences in visual-spatial ability: The role of performance factors. *Memory and Cognition, 18,* 546–550.

Graves, M. F. & Cooke, C. L. (1980). Effects of previewing difficult short stories for high school students. *Research on Reading in Secondary Schools, 6,* 38–54, 256–80.

Graves, M. F., Cooke, C. L., & Laberge, M. J. (1983). Effects of previewing difficult short stories on low ability junior high school students' comprehension, recall and attitudes. *Reading Research Quarterly, 18*(3), 262–276.

Graves, M. F., & Slater, W. H. (1987, April). *Development of reading vocabularies on rural disadvantaged students, intercity disadvantaged students, and middle class suburban students.* Paper presented at the AERA conference, Washington, DC.

Greene, J. P., & Winters, M. (2002). *Civic report #31: Public high school graduation rates.* Manhattan Institute. Retrieved on February 2, 2008, from http://www.manhattan-institute.org/html/cr_31.htm

Greene, J. P., & Winters, M. (2006). *Civic report #48: Leaving boys behind: Public high school graduation rates.* Manhattan Institute. Retrieved on February 2, 2008, from http://www.manhattan-institute.org/html/cr_48.htm

Grossen, B. (2000). *What does it mean to be a research-based profession?* University of Oregon. Retrieved April 22, 2008, from http://www.uoregon.edu/~bgrossen/pubs/resprf.htm

Gurian, M., Henley, E,, & Trueman, T. (2001). *Boys and girls learn differently!* San Francisco: Jossey-Bass.

Gurian, M., & Stevens, K. (2005). *The minds of boys: Saving our sons from falling behind in school and life.* Indianapolis: Jossey Bass.'

Guzzetti, B. J., Snyder, T. E., & Glass, G. V. (1993). Promoting conceptual change in science. *Reading Research Quarterly, 28*(2), 117–155.

Haberman, M. (1995). *Star teachers of children in poverty.* West Lafayettte, IN: Kappa Delta Pi.

Haggerty, S. (1991). Gender and school science: Achievement and participation in Canada. *Alberta Journal of Educational Research, 3,* 195–208.

Hallahan, D., & Kauffman, J. (1994). From mainstreaming to collaborative consultation. In J. Kauffman & D. Hallahan (Eds.), *The illusion of full inclusion* (pp. 3–17). Austin, TX: PRO-ED.

Haney, W., Madaus, G., Abrams, L., Wheelock, A., Miao, J., & Gruia, I. (2004). *The education pipeline in the United States, 1970–2000.* Boston College: National Board on Educational Testing and Public Policy.

Harlan, W. (2003). *Enhancing inquiry through formative assessment.* San Francisco Institute for Inquiry. Retrieved on January 8, 2008, from http://www.exploratorium.edu/ifi/resources/harlen_monograph.pdf

Hayes, D., & Tierney, R. (1982). Developing readers' knowledge through analogy. *Reading Research Quarterly, 17*(2), 256–80.

Hibbard, M., & Yakimowski, M. (1997). *Assessment in Connecticut: A partnership to improve student performance-connecting state-level assessment and classroom practices.* Cheshire, CT: Connecticut Association for Supervision and Curriculum Development.

House Resolution 6: Improving America's Schools Act. (1994). Retrieved April 22, 2008, from http://www.ed.gov/legislation/ESEA/toc.html

Howard, B. C. (1987). *Learning to persist: Persisting to learn [training program].* Washington, DC: Mid-Atlantic Center for Race Equity, American University.

Hulme, M. A. (1988). Mirror, mirror on the wall: Biased reflections in textbooks and instructional materials. In A. Carellie (Ed.), *Sex equity in education* (pp. 187–206). Springfield, IL: Charles C. Thomas.

Hunsader, P. (2002). Why boys fail—and what we can do about it. *Principal, 82*(2), 52–55.

Hutchins, P. (1989). *The doorbell rang.* Parsippany, NJ: Pearson Learning.

Hyerle, D. (2000). *A field guide to visual tools.* Alexandria, VA: Association for Supervision and Curriculum.

Idol, L., Nevin, A., & Paolucci-Whitcomb, P. (1994). *Collaborative consultation.* Austin, TX: PRO-ED.

Individuals With Disabilities Education Act Amendments. (1997). Pub. L. No 105–17.

International Center for Educational Accountability. (2007). Retrieved on January 2, 2008, from http://icea.communityisoft.com

Jalongo, M. R. (1994). *Helping children cope with relocation.* Retrieved June 13, 2008 from www.questia.com/googleScholar.qst?docId=5002220957

James, A. (2007). *Teaching the male brain: How boys think, feel, and learn in school.* Thousand Oaks, CA: Corwin Press.

Johnson, C. (2006). *Unmasking the truth: Teaching diverse student populations.* National Association of Elementary School Principals. Retrieved January 6, 2008, from http://www.naesp.org/ContentLoad.do?contentId=1845

Johnson, D. W., & Johnson, R. (1989). *Cooperation and competition: Theory and research.* Edina, MN: Interaction Book Co.

Johnson, G. M. (1999). Inclusive education: Fundamental instructional strategies and considerations. *Preventing School Failure, 43*(2), 72–78.

Joos, M. (1972). The styles of the five clocks. In R. Abrahams & R. Troike (Eds.), *Language and Cultural Diversity in American Education.* Englewood, NJ: Prentice Hall.

Kafer, K. (2007). *Taking the boy crisis in education seriously: How school choice can boost achievement among boys and girls.* Washington, DC: Women for School Choice, a Project of the Independent Women's Forum (Position Paper No. 604).

Kimura, D. (2002). Sex differences in the brain. *Scientific American.* Retrieved February 22, 2008, from http://www.sciam.com/article.cfm?articleID=00018E9D-1D06–8E49809EC588EEDF

Kindlon, D., & Thompson, M. (1999). *Raising Cain: Protecting the emotional life of boys.* New York: Ballantine.

King, A. (1994). Guiding knowledge construction in the classroom: Effects of teaching children how to question and how to explain. *American Educational Research Journal, 3*(12), 338–368.

Klausmeier, H. J. (1985). *Educational psychology* (5th ed.). New York: Harper & Row.

Kolb, A., & Kolb, D. A. (2001). *Experiential learning theory bibliography 1971–2001.* Boston: McBer and Co.

Kommer, D. (2006). *Creating gender-friendly middle school classrooms.* Middle Matters. Retrieved May 5, 2008, from http://www.naesp.org/ContentLoad.do?contentId=1851

Kuykendall, C. (1991). *Improving black student achievement [training program].* Chevy Chase, MD: Mid-Atlantic Equity Consortium.

Kuykendall, C. (2004). *From rage to hope: Strategies for reclaiming Black and Hispanic students* (2nd ed.). Bloomington, IN: Solution Tree.

Labinowicz, E. (1980). *The Piaget primer: Thinking learning and teaching.* Menlo Park, CA: Addision-Wesley.

Lambert, M. (1986). Knowing, doing, and teaching multiplication. *Cognition and Instruction, 3,* 305–342.

Lee, D., Harrison, C., & Black, P. (2004). *Teachers developing assessment for learning: Impact on student achievement.* Retrieved April 23, 2008, from http://www .eric.ed.gov/ERICWebPortal/custom/portlets/recordDetails/detailmini.jsp?_nfpb= true&_&ERICExtSearch_SearchValue_0=EJ680303&ERICExtSearch_SearchType _0=no&accno=EJ680303

Legal Information Institute. (n.d.). Stewart B. McKinney Homeless Assistance Act 1987. Retrieved April 23, 2008, from http://www.law.cornell.edu/uscode/ 42/usc_sec_42_00011411—000-.html

Letrello, T. M., & Miles, D. D. (2003). Transition from middle school to high school: Students with and without learning disabilities share their perceptions. *The Clearing House* (March/April 2003), 212–214.

Lin, J., & Chen, X. (2007). *Exploring creative ways to enhance girls' learning: Learning from all girl schools around the world.* Retrieved April 23, 2008, from http:// www.unicef.org/china/P2_LIN_Jing_paper.pdf

Lingard, B., Martino, W., Mills, M., & Bahr, M. (2002). *Addressing the educational needs of boys.* Australian Government Department of Education, Science and Training. Retrieved May 1, 2008, from http://www.dest.gov.au/sectors/school_education/ publications_resources/profiles/addressing_educational_needs_of_boys.htm

Lloyd, S. (2007). Gender gap in graduation. *Education Week.* Retrieved February 19, 2008, from http://www.edweek.org/rc/articles/2007/07/05/sow0705.h26.html

Lorenzen, M. (2003). *Active learning and library instruction.* Retrieved January 31, 2008, from http://www.libraryinstruction.com/active.html

Lovelace, M. (2005). Meta-analysis of experimental research based on the Dunn and Dunn model. *The Journal of Educational Research, 98*(3), 176–183.

Marzano, R. (1998). *A theory-based meta-analysis of research on instruction.* Aurora, CO: Mid-Continent Regional Educational Laboratory.

Marzano, R. (2001a). *Research-based strategies for every teacher.* Aurora, CO: Mid-Continent Regional Educational Laboratory.

Marzano, R. (2001b). *What works in classroom instruction.* Aurora, CO: Mid-Continental Regional Educational Laboratory.

Marzano, R. (2003). *What works in schools: Translating research into action.* Alexandria, VA: Association for Supervision and Curriculum Development.

Marzano, R. (2004). *Building background knowledge for academic achievement: Research on what works in schools.* Alexandria, VA: Association for Supervision and Curriculum Development.

Marzano, R. (2006). *Classroom assessment and grading that work.* Alexandria, VA: Association for Supervision and Curriculum Development.

Marzano, R. (2007). *The art and science of teaching: A comprehensive framework for effective instruction.* Alexandria, VA: Association for Supervision and Curriculum Development.

Marzano, R., Gaddy, B. B., & Dean, C. (2000). *What works in classroom instruction.* Aurora, CO: Mid-Continental Regional Educational Laboratory.

Marzano & Haystead (2008). *Making standards useful in the classroom.* Alexandria, VA: Association for Supervision and Curriculum Development.

Marzano, R., Norford, J., Paynter, D., Pickering, D. J., & Gaddy, B. (2001). *A handbook for classroom instruction that works.* Alexandria, VA: Association for Supervision and Curriculum Development.

Marzano, R., & Pickering, D. J. (2005). *Building academic vocabulary: Teacher's manual.* Alexandria, VA: Association for Supervision and Curriculum Development.

Marzano, R., Pickering, D. J., & Pollock, J. (2001). *Classroom instruction that works.* Alexandria, VA: Association for Supervision and Curriculum Development.

Massell, D. (2000). *The district role in building capacity: Four strategies.* Retrieved May 4, 2008, from http://www.doe.state.de.us/Programs/si/files/District%20Role%20Building%20Capacity.pdf

McKinney, K. (2008). *Active learning.* Illinois State University. Center for Teaching, Learning and Technology. Retrieved May 3, 2008, from http://www.teachtech.ilstu.edu/additional/active.php

Mead, S. (2006). *The evidence suggests otherwise: The truth about boys and girls.* Washington, DC: Education Sector.

Miami Museum of Science. (2001). *Alternative assessment.* Retrieved June 22, 2008 from http://www.miamisci.org/ph/lpexamine1.html

Mid-Atlantic Equity Center. (1993). *Beyond Title IX: Gender equity issues in schools.* Chevy Chase, MD: Author.

Mid-Atlantic Equity Center. (1999). *Adolescent boys: Statistics and trends [fact sheet].* Chevy Chase, MD: Author.

Miller, J. (1993). Trouble in mind. *Mind and brain* (pp. 137–138). New York: W. H. Freeman.

Minstrell, J. (1989). Teaching science for understanding. In L. B. Resnick & L. Klopfer (Eds.), *Toward the thinking curriculum* (pp. 129–149). Alexandria, VA: Association for Supervision and Curriculum Development.

Mishel, L., Roy J. (2006). *Rethinking high school graduation rates and trends.* WA D.C.: Economic Policy Institute.

Montgomery County Public Schools. (1997). *Performance-based assessment tasks for social studies.* Retrieved June 22, 2008 from http://www.montgomeryschoolsmd.org/curriculum/socialstd/MSPAP/Games2.html

Munns, G., et al. (2006). *Motivation and engagement of boys: Evidence-based teaching practices (Appendices).* Australian Government Department of Education, Science and Training. Retrieved April 30, 2008, from http://www.dest.gov.au/sectors/research_sector/publications_resources/profiles/motivation_engagement_boys.htm

Nagy, W. E., & Herman, P. A. (1984). *Limitations of vocabulary instruction* (Tech. Rep. No. 326). Urbana, IL: University of Illinois, Center for the Study of Reading. (ERIC Document Service No. ED248498).

National Center for Children in Poverty. (2007). *Basic facts about low-income children in the United States.* Retrieved January 1, 2007, from http://www.nccp.org/publications/pub_762.html

National Center for Children in Poverty. (2007). *Testimony at the House Ways and Means Committee hearing on the economic and societal costs of poverty.* Retrieved January 1, 2007, from http://www.americanprogress.org/issues/2007/01/holzer_testimony.html

National Center for Educational Statistics. (2004). *Trends in educational equity of girls and women.* Retrieved February 23, 2008, from http://nces.ed.gov/pubs2005/equity/Sections5.asp

National Center for Education Statistics. (2005a). *The nation's report card: NAEP 2004 trends.* Washington, DC: U.S. Department of Education. Retrieved December 28, 2007, from http://www.nces.ed.gov/nationsreportcard/pdf/main2005/2005464.pdf

National Center for Education Statistics. (2005b). *Trends in educational equity of girls and women 2004.* Retrieved June 12, 2008 from http://nces.ed.gov.pubs2005/equity/

National Center for Education Statistics. (2007). Washington, DC: U.S. Department of Education. Retrieved December 15, 2007, from http:www.http://nces.ed.gov/

National Center for Homeless Education. (n.d.). *Data on homeless children and youth.* Retrieved May 4, 2008, from http://www.serve.org/nche

National Center for the Improvement of Educational Assessment. (2006). *Incorporating growth models into AYP determinations: NCME 2006 growth progression materials.* Retrieved January 1, 2008, from http://www.nciea.org/

National Center for Women and Information Technology. (2007). *By the numbers: Women and information technology.* Retrieved June 13, 2008 from ncwit .org/pdf/Stat_sheet_2007.pdf

National Clearinghouse for English Language Acquisition. (2002). *Elementary and secondary LEP enrollment growth and top languages.* Retrieved May 3, 2008, from http://www.ncela.gwu.edu/pubs/reports/state-data/2000/index.htm

National Commission on Teaching and America's Future. (1996). *What matters most: Teaching for America's future.* New York: National Commission on Teaching and America's Future. Retrieved May 4, 2008, from http://www.nctaf.org/documents/WhatMattersMost.pdf

National Council for the Social Studies. (2002). *Curriculum guidelines for social studies teaching and learning.* Retrieved January 25, 2008, from http://www.socialstudies .org/positions/curriculum

National Council of Teachers of English. (2002). *Guidelines for gender-fair use of language.* Retrieved January 31, 2008, from http://www.ncte.org/about/over/positions/category/lang/107647.htm

National Governors Association. (2005). *Graduation counts: A report of the national governors association task force on state high school graduation data.* Washington D.C.: Author.

Nelson, K. (2000, February). Measuring the intangibles. *Classroom Leadership: A Newsletter for K–12 Classroom Teachers, 3*(5), 1, 8.

Nelson-Le Gall, S. (1985). Help-seeking behavior in learning. *Review of Research in Education, 12,* 55–90.

Nesbit, J. C., & Adesope, O. O. (2006). Learning with concept and knowledge maps: A meta-analysis. *Review of Educational Research, 76*(3), 413–448.

Neu, T. W., & Weinfeld, R. (2007). *Helping boys succeed in school: A practical guide for parents and teachers.* Waco, TX: Prufrock Press.

Newkirk, T. (2002). *Misreading masculinity: Boys, literacy and popular culture.* Portsmouth, NH: Heinemann.

Noble, C. & Bradford, W. (2000). *Getting it right for boys . . . and girls.* New York: Routledge.

North Central Regional Educational Laboratory. (1997). *Critical issue: Ensuring equity with alternative assessments.* Retrieved June 13, 2008, from http://www.ncrel.org/sdrs/areas/issues/methods/assment/as800.htm

Northwest Regional Educational Laboratory. (2001). *Meeting the needs of immigrant students.* Retrieved January 5, 2008, from http:/www.nwrel.org/cnorse/booklets/immigration/index.html

Northwest Regional Educational Laboratory. (2007). *Toolkit98.* Retrieved June 12, 2008 from http://www.nwrel.org/assessment/toolkit98.php

Nunley, K. (2000). In defense of oral defense. *Classroom Leadership: A Newsletter for K–12 Classroom Teachers,* February, 6.

Nunley, K. (2004). *Layered curriculum: The practical solution for teachers with more than one student in their classrooms* (2nd ed.). Amherst, NH: Brains.org.

Nuthall, G. (1999). The way students learn: Acquiring knowledge from an integrated science and social studies unit. *Elementary School Journal, 99*(4), 303–341.

Nuthall, G., & Alton-Lee, A. (1995). Assessing classroom learning: How students use their knowledge and experience to answer classroom achievement test questions in science and social studies. *American Educational Research Journal, 32*(1), 185–257.

Oakes, J. (1985). *Keeping track: How schools structure inequality.* New Haven, CT: Yale University Press.

Office for Standards in Education. (2003). *Boys' achievement in secondary schools* (HMI 1659). Retrieved February 22, 2008, from http://www.ofsted.gov.uk/assets/3316.pdf

Ogle, D. S. (1986). K-W-L group instructional strategy. In A. Palinscar, D. S. Ogle, B. E Jones, & E. G. Carr (Eds.), *Teaching reading as thinking: Teleconference resource guide* (pp. 11–17). Alexandria, VA: Association for Supervision and Curriculum Development.

Olson, M., Chalmers, L., & Hoover, J. (1997). Attitudes and attributes of general education teachers identified as effective inclusionists. *Remedial and Special Education, 18*(1), 28–35.

Organization for Economic Cooperation and Development. (2005). *Formative assessment: Improving learning in secondary classrooms.* Retrieved January 3, 2008, from http://www.oecd.org/dataoecd/19/31/35661078.pdf

Ovando, C., & Collier, V. (1998). *Bilingual and ESL classrooms: Teaching in multicultural contexts.* Boston: McGraw-Hill.

Page, R. (1991). *Lower track classrooms: A curricular and cultural perspective.* New York: Teachers College Press.

Patchen, T. (2005, Summer). Prioritizing participation: Five things that every teacher needs to know to prepare recent immigrant adolescents for classroom participation. *Multicultural Education,* 43–47.

Payne, R. (1995). *Poverty: A framework for understanding and working with students and adults from poverty.* Baytown, TX: RFT Publishing.

PBS Parents. (2007). *Boys in school: Logical solutions.* Retrieved February 22, 2008, from http://www.pbs.org/parents/raisingboys/sch00105.html

Piaget, J. (1968). *Judgment and reasoning in the child.* (M. Warden, Trans.). Totowa, NJ: Littlefield & Adams.

Pike, K. (1995, Fall). A comparison of traditional and authentic assessments. *Teaching Exceptional Children,* 15–20.

Pike, K., & Salend, S. (1995, Fall). Authentic assessment strategies: Alternatives to norm-referenced testing. *Teaching Exceptional Children,* 15–20.

Pillard, N. (2007). *What's sex got to do with it? Sex equality and the single-sex movement.* Retrieved April 28, 2008, from http://law.usc.edu/assets/docs/Pillard.pdf

Pollack, W. (1998). *Real boys: Rescuing our sons from the myths of boyhood.* New York: Random House.

Pressley, M., Allington, R., Wharton-McDonald, R., Collins-Block, C., & Morrow, L. (2001). *Learning to read: Lessons from exemplary first-grade classrooms.* New York: Guilford.

Pressley, M., Wood, E., Woloshyn, V. E., Martin, V., King, A., & Menke, D. (1992). Strategies that improve children's memory and comprehension of text. *The Elementary School Journal, 90*(1), 3–32.

Ramirez, M. III, & Casteneda, A. (1974). Cultural democracy: *Bicognitive development and education.* New York: Academic Press.

Revilla, A. T., and Sweeney, Y. D. (1997). *High performing/high poverty schools.* Retrieved June 13, 2008 from www.idra.org/IDRA_Newsletter/June_-_July_1997_High_-_Performing_High_Poverty_Schools/

Richards, M. (2005). *The effects of tiered lessons on learning gain in a secondary freshman earth science course, as measured by assessment performance.* DAI-A 66/07. Retrieved December 15, 2007, from http://proquest.umi.com/pqdweb?index=1&did=954013561&SrchMode

Roberts, J., & Inman, T. (2007). *Strategies for differentiating instruction: Best practices for the classroom.* Waco, TX: Prufrock Press.

Robinson, D. H., & Keiwra, K. A. (1996). Visual argument: Graphic organizers are superior to outlines in improving learning from text. *Journal of Educational Psychology, 87*(3), 455–467.

Roschelle, J. (1997). *Learning interactive environments: Prior knowledge and new experience.* Institute for Inquiry. Retrieved April 30, 2008, from http://www.exploratorium.edu/IFI/resources/museumeducation/priorknowledge.html

Rousseau, J. J. (1762). *Emile: or, on education* (trans. 1979). New York: Basic Books.

Rovee-Collier, C. (1995). Time windows in cognitive development. *Developmental Psychology, 31*(2), 147–169.

Sadker, D., & Sadker, M. (2001). Gender bias: From colonial America to today's classrooms. In J. Banks & C. Banks (Eds.), *Multicultural education: Issues and perspectives* (pp. 135–169). New York: John Wiley.

Sadker, M., & Sadker, D. (1994). *Failing at fairness: How our schools cheat girls.* New York: Touchstone.

Salvner, G., Brown, J. E., & Stephens, E. C. (Eds.). (1998). *United in diversity: Using multicultural young adult literature in the classroom.* Urbana, IL: National Council of Teachers of English.

Sandefur, S. J., Watson, S. W., & Johnston, L. B. (2007, Spring). Literacy development, science curriculum, and the adolescent English language learner. *Multicultural Education,* 41–50.

Schmoker, M. (2001). *The results fieldbook: Practical strategies from dramatically improved schools.* Alexandria, VA: Association for Supervision and Curriculum Development.

Schumm, J. S., Vaughn, S., & Sobol, M. C. (1997). Are they getting it? How to monitor student understanding in inclusive classrooms. *Intervention in School and Clinic, 3,* 168–171.

Seidel, S. (1991). *Collaborative assessment conferences for the consideration of project work* [working paper]. Cambridge, MA: Project Zero, Harvard Graduate School of Education.

Shade, B. J. (1989). *Culture, style, and the educative process.* Springfield, IL: Charles C. Thompson.

Shavel, J. P. (1999). Social studies. In G. Cawelti (Ed.), *Handbook on research on improving student achievement* (2nd ed.). Arlington, VA: Educational Research Service.

Shrock, K. Kathy Shrock's guide to educators: *Assessment rubrics.* Retrieved June 22, 2008 from http://school.discoveryeducation.com/schrockguide/assess.html

Shulman, L. (1987). Knowledge and teaching: Foundations of the new reform. *Harvard Educational Review, 57,* 1–22.

Slavin, R. (1987). Ability grouping and student achievement in the elementary schools: A best-evidence synthesis. *Review of Educational Research, 57,* 293–336.

Slavin, R. (1990). *Cooperative learning.* Englewood Cliffs, NJ: Prentice Hall.

Smith, J. B., Lee, V. E., & Newmann, F. M. (2001). *Instruction and achievement in Chicago elementary schools.* Chicago: Consortium on Chicago School Research.

Smith, M., & Wilhelm, J. (2002). *Reading don't fix no Chevys.* Portsmouth, NH: Heinemann.

Snow, C., Burns, S., & Griffin, P. (1998). *Preventing reading difficulties in young children.* Washington, DC: National Academy Press.

Sommers, C. H. (2000). *The war against boys: How misguided feminism is harming our young men.* New York: Simon & Schuster.

Southern Regional Education Board (SREB) (2002). *Opening doors to the future: Preparing low-achieving middle grades students to succeed in high school.* Atlanta, GA: Author.

State of Queensland, Australia. (2002). *The new basics project/productive pedagogies: Background knowledge.* Retrieved January 14, 2008, from http://education.qld.gov.au/corporate/newbasics/html/pedagogies/connect/con2a.html

Stevens, K. (1980). The effect of background knowledge on the reading comprehension of ninth graders. *Journal of Reading Behavior, 12*(2), 151–154.

Stevens, K. (1982). Can we improve reading by teaching background information? *Journal of Reading, 25,* 326–29.

Stiggins, R. J. (1994). *Student-centered classroom assessment.* New York: Merrill.

Stiggins, R. J. (2005). *Student-involved classroom assessment* (4th ed.). Upper Saddle River, NJ: Prentice Hall.

Stiggins, R. J. (2000). *Student-involved classroom assessment.* Upper Saddle River, NJ: Prentice Hall.

Strangman, N., & Hall, T. (2004). *Background knowledge.* National Center on Accessing the General Curriculum. Retrieved January 10, 2008, from http://www.cast.org/publications/ncac/ncac_backknowledge.html

Strong, J. (2007). *Qualities of effective teachers.* Alexandria, VA: Association for Supervision and Curriculum Development.

Strong, R., Silver, H., Perini, M., & Tuculescu, G. (2002). *Reading for academic success: Powerful strategies for struggling, average, and advanced readers, grades 7–12.* Thousand Oaks, CA: Corwin Press.

Subotnik, R., & LeBlanc, G. (2001). Teaching gifted students in a multicultural society. In J. A. Banks & C. M. Banks (Eds.), *Multicultural education: Issues and perspectives* (pp. 353–376). New York: John Wiley.

Sylwester, R. (1995). *A celebration of neurons: An educator's guide to the human brain.* Alexandria, VA: Association for Supervision and Curriculum Development.

Sylwester, R. (2000). *A biological brain in a cultural classroom.* Thousand Oaks, CA: Corwin Press.

Tannenbaum, J. (1996). *Practical ideas on alternative assessment for ESL students.* Center for Applied Linguistics. Retrieved June 12, 2008 from http://www.cal.org/resources/Digest/tannen01.html

Taylor, D., & Lorimer, M. (2003). Helping boys succeed. *Educational Leadership, 60*(4), 68–70.

Teachers 21. (2007). *Three critical actions for promoting education equity. Reshaping the profession of teaching.* Retrieved February 20, 2008, from http://teachers21.org/#

Tharp, R. (1994). Intergroup differences among Native Americans in socialization and child cognition: An ethnogenetic analysis. In P. Greenfield and R. Cocking (Eds.), *Cross-cultural roots of minority child development* (pp. 87–105). Hillsdale, NJ: Lawrence Erlbaum.

Thomas, W. E., & Collier, V. P. (1997). *School effectiveness for language minority students.* Washington, DC: National Clearinghouse for Bilingual Education.

Tovey, R. (1995). A narrowly gender-based model of learning may end up cheating all students. *Harvard Education Letter, 9,* 3–6.

Ulmer, M. B. (2001, Spring). Self-grading for formative assessment in problem-based learning. *Academic Exchange Quarterly, 5,* 68–74.

Uniserve. (2006). *Alternative strategies for science teaching and assessment.* Retrieved June 12, 2008 from http://science.uniserve.edu.au/school/support/strategy.html

U.S. Census Bureau. (2001). *Poverty: 2000 highlights.* Retrieved May 4, 2008, from http://www.census.gov/hhes/www/poverty/poverty00/pov00hi.html

U.S. Department of Education. (2007). *The nation's report card.* National Center for Education Statistics. Retrieved January 1, 2008, from http://nces.ed.gov/nationsreportcard/naep2008.asp

U.S. Department of Education, National Center for Education Statistics. (2006). *Public elementary and secondary students, staff, schools, and school districts: School Year 2003–04* (NCES 2006–307).

U.S. Department of Education, National Center for Educational Statistics. (1998). *Statistical analysis report: State survey on racial and ethnic classifications.* Retrieved May 4, 2008, from http://nces.ed.gov/pubsearch/pubsinfo.asp?pubid=98034

U.S. Department of Education, National Center for Educational Statistics. (2001a). *Overview of public elementary and secondary schools and districts: School year 1999–2000.* Retrieved May 4, 2008, from http://www.nces.ed.gov/pubs2001/overview/

U.S. Department of Education, National Center for Educational Statistics. (2001b). Public school student, staff and graduate counts by state: School year 1999–2000. *Education Statistics Quarterly.* Retrieved May 4, 2008, from http://nces.ed.gov/pubsearch/pubsinfo.asp?pubid=2002348

U.S. Department of Education, National Center for Educational Statistics. (n.d.). *National assessment of educational progress: Reading.* Retrieved May 4, 2008, from http://nces.ed.gov/nationsreportcard/reading/

U.S. Department of Education, National Institute for Literacy. (2000). *Reading: Know what works.* Washington, DC: Author.

U.S. Department of Education, Office for Civil Rights. (2006). *Nondiscrimination on the basis of sex in education programs or activities receiving federal financial assistance.* Retrieved May 4, 2008, from http://www.ed.gov/legislation/FedRegister/finrule/2006-4/102506a.html

U.S. Department of Education, Office of Special Education and Rehabilitative Services. (2000). *Twenty-second annual report to congress on the implementation of the Individuals with Disabilities Education Act.* Retrieved April 23, 2008, from http://www.ed.gov/about/reports/annual/osep/2000/execsumm.html

U.S. Department of Education. (1997a). *America reads challenge: Evidence that tutoring works.* Retrieved April 23, 2008, from http://www.ed.gov/inits/americareads/resourcekit/miscdocs/tutorwork.html

U.S. Department of Education. (1997b). *Assessment of student performance: Studies of educational reform.* Retrieved May 4, 2008, from http://www.ed.gov/pubs/SER/ASP/

U.S. Department of Education. (2007). *Response to intervention—Special education research.* Retrieved May 4, 2008, from http://www.ed.gov/programs/specedintervention/legislation.html

U.S. Department of Health and Human Services. (2007). *The 2007 HHS poverty guidelines.* Retrieved May 4, 2008, from http://aspe.hhs.gov/poverty/07poverty.shtml

Vacca, R. (1981). *Content area reading.* Boston: Little, Brown.

Vaughn, S., & Wanzek, J. (2007). *National Center for Learning Disabilities.* Retrieved May 4, 2008, from http://www.ncld.org/content/view/1226

Viadero, D. (2007). *ADHD experts fear brain-growth study being misconstrued.* Retrieved May 4, 2008, from http://www.edweek.org/ew/articles/2007/12/05/14adhd.h27.html?print=1

Viadero. D. (2006). Concern over gender gaps shifting to boys. *Education Week, 25*(27), 1, 16–17.

Vissing, Y. M. (1996). *Out of sight, out of mind.* Lexington: University Press of Kentucky.

Walberg, H., & Paik, S. (2005). Making giftedness productive. In R. Sternberg & J. Davidson (Eds.), *Conceptions of giftedness* (2nd ed.) (pp. 395–410). Cambridge: Cambridge University Press.

Webb, M. (1990). *Multicultural education in elementary and secondary schools*. ERIC Digest #67. Retrieved April 23, 2008, from http://www.ericdigests.org/pre-9218/secondary.htm

Wheelock, A. (1992). *Crossing the tracks: How untracking can save America's schools*. New York: New Press.

Wiggins, G. (2000). *Educative assessment: Designing assessments to inform and improve student performance*. San Francisco: Jossey-Bass.

Wiggins, G., & McTighe, J. (1998). *Understanding by design*. Alexandria, VA: Association for Supervision and Curriculum Development.

Wiggins, G., & McTighe, J. (2005). *Understanding by design* (2nd ed.). Alexandria, VA: Association for Supervision and Curriculum Development.

Williams, B. (2006, Fall). Lessons along the cultural spectrum. *Journal of Staff Development, 27*, 10–14.

Willis, J. (2006). *Research-based strategies to ignite student learning*. Arlington, VA: Association for Supervision and Curriculum Development.

Wilson, G. (2003). *Using the national healthy school standard to raise boys' achievement*. United Kingdom Department for Education and Skills. Retrieved May 4, 2008, from http://www.standards.dfes.gov.uk/genderandachievement/nhss_boys_achievement2.pdf?version=1

Wininger, S., & Norman, A. (2005). Teacher candidates' exposure to formative assessment in psychology textbooks: A content analysis. *Educational Assessment, 10* (1), 19–37.

Witkin, H. A., Moore, C. A., Goodenough, D. R., & Cox, P. W. (1977). Field-dependent and field-independent cognitive styles and their educational implications. *Review of Educational Research, 47*, 1–64.

Woodward, A., & Elliot, D. (1990). Textbook use and teacher professionalism. In D. Elliot & A. Woodward (Eds.), *Textbooks and schooling in the United States* (89th Yearbook of the National Society for the Study of Education) (pp. 178–193). Chicago: University of Chicago Press.

World Almanac (Ed.). (2008). *World almanac for kids*. New York: World Almanac.

Wormelli, R. (2006). *Fair isn't always equal: Assessing and grading in the differentiated classroom*. Portland, ME: Stenhouse.

Younger, M., & Warrington, M. (2005). *Raising boys' achievement*. Retrieved May 3, 2008, from http://www.dfes.gov.uk/research/data/uploadfiles/RR636.pdf

Zemelman, S., Daniels, H., & Hyde, A. (1998). *Best practice: New standards for teaching and learning in America's schools*. (2nd ed). Portsmouth, NH: Heinemann.

Zemelman, S., Daniels, H., & Hyde, A. (2005). *Best practice: New standards for teaching and learning in America's schools* (3rd Ed.). Portsmouth, NH: Heinemann.

Zirkel, S. (2002). Is there a place for me? Role models and academic identity among white students and students of color. *Teachers College Record, 104*(2), 357–376.

Index